READY
SET
TEACH

Crafting a Learning-Ready Curriculum for Every Classroom

Dr Janelle Wills

 A catalogue record for this book is available from the National Library of Australia

© 2024 Grift Education. All rights reserved.

This work is copyright. Apart from fair dealings for the purposes of study, research, criticism or review, or as permitted under the Copyright Act 1968 (Cth), no part should be reproduced, transmitted, communicated or recorded, in any form or by any means, without the prior written permission of the copyright owner.

grifteducation

PO Box 3160 Mentone East, Victoria 3194, Australia
Phone: (03) 8686 9077

Website: www.grifteducation.com

Email: orders@grifteducation.com

Code: GE8388

ISBN: 9781923198388 (Paperback)

ISBN: 9781923198999 (eBook)

Printed in Australia

About the Author

Dr Janelle Wills is an experienced educator with over 40 years of teaching and leadership roles in Australian education. She has been influential in promoting positive change in schools and sectors across the country.

Dr Wills holds a PhD that explored self-efficacy and reading development. She has also made significant contributions to various aspects of education, such as special education, gifted education, assessment and feedback. Her research has enhanced and informed these areas, revealing effective teaching methods and techniques.

For over ten years, she has worked alongside Dr Robert Marzano to support schools in implementing his evidence-based strategies in an Australian context. Much of this work has involved assisting school leaders and their teacher teams to develop collaborative school cultures, establish highly effective teaching practices, develop a guaranteed and viable curriculum and implement standard-referenced reporting processes in a consistent manner. At this time, Dr Wills is the only person in Australia certified to provide this support.

Dr Wills is also a writer, having authored and co-authored many articles and books. Some of her works include *Thinking Protocols for Learning, Transformative Collaboration: Five Commitments for Leading a PLC, A Handbook for High Reliability Schools* and *The New Art and Science of Teaching Reference Guide*.

As a strong supporter of the teaching profession, Dr Wills ardently encourages educators to use research through action research and reflective practice. Her dedication to ongoing learning keeps her at the cutting edge of educational innovation, ensuring that her work is dynamic and up to date.

To book Janelle for professional development, contact janelle@jweducation.com.au

To access Grift Education's Digital support and tools for *Ready, Set, Teach* please scan the QR Code:

Foreword

Anyone at the frontline of education knows the undeniable truth that teaching is a complex, demanding occupation. In fact, renowned educational psychologist Lee Schulman (2004) described classroom teaching as 'perhaps the most complex, most challenging, and most demanding, subtle, nuanced, and frightening activity that our species has even invented.' (p. 504).

The demands and complexity of teaching have only continued to increase in the twenty years since Schulman made this observation and little impactful work has been done to accommodate for these changes. Accelerating societal demands, mounting administrative responsibilities, increasing accountability requirements and an ever-expanding spectrum of diverse student learning needs have resulted in a profound intensification and escalation of the multifaceted demands on educators. Teachers today are required to meet the changing complexity of their responsibilities which range from knowledge and curriculum guru, counsellor and confidant, moral and cultural compass, life coach and cheerleader, to name a few.

For decades, schools and educators have been concerned about curriculum overcrowding, with research indicating it contributes significantly to their workload and stress. In a recent review from teachers, leaders and professional associations, responses such as 'overcrowded', 'overloaded', 'cluttered' and 'promoting a tick-box approach to teaching' were received (Australian Primary Principals Association [APPA], 2020).

The pressure to cover all content has led to a learning experience that can feel fragmented and overloaded. Frustrated teachers report that they are 'skimming' the surface or 'bouncing' between topics, unable to 'dig deeper' in their quest to 'cover all the content'. The undesired, but ultimate, consequence of this approach is a reduction in the quality of learning, disengagement in learning amongst students and increased frustration of educators. Teachers are often forced through necessity to make individual decisions about what content to prioritise, leading to a 'learning lotto' – potentially inconsistent learning experiences and outcomes for students in different classrooms.

Even when the problem is well known, can be easily articulated and its impact felt daily, inertia to changing the status quo or solving the problem is often the result of not knowing how to start or what process to use. Lacking a clear process to overcome the problem can discourage change, even when people are acutely aware that there is a problem. A key component of the role of school leaders is to do everything in their power to reduce this complexity for educators. One clear way of doing this is by ensuring that educators have a clear and coherent process for successfully overcoming the debilitating impact of an overcrowded curriculum and are given privileged time required to implement the process.

In her book *Ready, Set, Teach*, Dr Janelle Wills resolves this impasse for school leaders and educators by delineating a research-informed process that provides them with a way of resolving the overcrowded curriculum dilemma.

Steeped in a comprehensive knowledge of the Australian education system, a nuanced awareness of curricula and assessment requirements and a wealth of practical experience working with schools, Dr Wills articulates a powerful and effective process which truly allows educators to work collaboratively to finally resolve the issue of the overcrowded curriculum. The logical and clearly articulated process she advocates in this easy-to-read book empowers schools to move from 'admiring the problem' to 'solving the problem'. By working collaboratively together through the process described, educators become curriculum experts and develop a 'learning-ready curriculum' that is primed for teachers to teach it and for students to learn it.

By following this step-by-step process to develop the learning-ready curriculum, educators gain clarity and reach agreement about curriculum expectations; they set priorities, they agree on time requirements to teach key concepts and they design learning pathways so that their students are ready to engage with a curriculum that allows time for deeper thinking and learning mastery.

I highly recommend this practical and insightful book to all school leaders and educators, not only for its accessible and jargon-free style, but for its genuine ability to resolve a dilemma that schools and educators have been grappling with from when curricula were first introduced. Dr Wills' research-informed blueprint not only provides schools with the clear and definitive process that produces an agreed-on schoolwide curriculum that is learning ready, but as equally important, liberates educators to allow them to become curriculum experts.

As curriculum experts, these educators possess a robust understanding of the curriculum. They are more effective at creating learning pathways that help students acquire the knowledge and skills for future learning success and they inspire learners to achieve excellence, fostering resilience, curiosity and a lifelong passion for learning.

Ready, Set, Teach empowers educators to cut through the curriculum clutter to enhance student learning.

Colin Sloper

Author & PLC Expert

Dedication

To all of the educators who have lamented about the lack of instructional time to adequately teach the content in mandated curriculum documents. Your frustrations and concerns are valid. May this book serve as one way of supporting you and the work of your collaborative teams.

In the process of writing this book, I came across the most beautiful poem called *Lessons of Another Kind* by Leslie Owen Wilson. For copyright reasons I can't include the poem but here is the link if you would like to read it. It's worth the time. https://thesecondprinciple.com/homepage/poetry-corner-poems-teaching-learning/lessons-another-kind

'Perhaps it is enough to say, I came to teach but learned instead' is the last line of the poem. It encapsulates so much of what it means to be a teacher and a continuous learner. Over my career, I have had the privilege of learning with and from so many extraordinary educators in a wide range of settings and contexts. All these experiences have shaped me and consequently the writing and content of this book.

Acknowledgement

I would like to acknowledge the leaders and teachers who I have worked with in the process of developing a guaranteed and viable curriculum over many years. This has included special schools, regional and rural schools, large metropolitan schools (primary and secondary) and networks of schools across the country. Through the process I have learned what works and doesn't work and where time is best spent.

Dr Robert J. Marzano has been a huge influence on my work, and I would like to acknowledge his vision and depth of research. He has always been a great support and inspiration and I thank him for entrusting me to represent his work. Along the way, I have also been fortunate enough to work with outstanding Australian thought leaders such as Gavin Grift and Colin Sloper. We have had endless conversations about the most effective ways to support collaborative teams as they work through the various challenges that can arise.

The vision for this book was for it to be a practical and concise resource to support educators working through the complexities of curriculum prioritisation. The diligent team at Grift Education, including Sam Himawan and Hillary Pan, ensured that the vision became a reality. Their meticulous attention to detail, thoughtful suggestions and tireless efforts were invaluable.

Finally, and in no way reflective of importance, I would like to acknowledge my family – my partner, Greg Hambrecht, for his love and encouragement; my son, Nathan, and his wife, Valerie; and my daughter, Hannah. They are always there to offer insights, acknowledgement of my achievements and love. Hannah is also a dedicated and caring teacher. She reminds me almost daily of the challenges teachers face and keeps me grounded, providing moral support and advice. And then, of course, there is my darling granddaughter, Evie, and my partner's effervescent granddaughter, Frankie. These two amazing girls have been at the forefront of my mind as I have written this book. Evie is about to turn three and Frankie will turn four a few months later. They both have a sparkle and zest for learning, and I hope that this book will help educators to understand that the Evies and Frankies of the world (and there are many) will enter classrooms in Foundation soon with a wealth of knowledge, curiosity and hunger to learn more. We need to be ready for them. Ready so that their learning doesn't stall, that they continue to be intrinsically motivated and empowered to do great things in the future.

Table of Contents

About the Author	i
Foreward	ii
Dedication	v
Acknowledgement	v
INTRODUCTION	**1**
Laying the foundation and establishing the 'Why'	2
Chapter 1: PRIORITISE CONTENT FOR LEARNING	**9**
Seductive shortcuts	10
Prioritisation steps	11
Conclusion	23
Final word	23
Planning questions	24
Chapter 2: IDENTIFY THE SKILLS, KNOWLEDGE AND DISPOSITIONS FOR THE PRIORITISED STANDARDS	**25**
Unpack the standard	25
Translate into learning goals	28
Undertake professional learning	30
Commit	30
Conclusion	31
Final word	31
Planning questions	32

Chapter 3: DETERMINE THE MOST ESSENTIAL PREREQUISITE KNOWLEDGE — 33

    Identify essential prerequisite skills and knowledge — 33

    Determine key academic vocabulary — 35

    Create pre-assessments and establish readiness levels — 39

    Consider enrichment and extension approaches — 41

    Conclusion — 44

    Final word — 45

    Planning questions — 45

Chapter 4: DISCUSS WAYS OF SHARING THE LEARNING PATHWAY WITH STUDENTS — 47

    Metacognition and self-regulatory behaviours — 47

    Create and communicate a clear learning pathway — 53

    Show the connection between class activities and learning goals — 58

    Use assessment as a tool for progress monitoring — 58

    Build routines for reflection and goal setting — 60

    Utilise student voice and feedback — 63

    Conclusion — 64

    Final word — 65

    Planning questions — 65

Glossary of Terms — 66

REFERENCES — 68

    APPENDIX A — 73

    APPENDIX B — 74

    APPENDIX C — 76

INTRODUCTION

'The hardest part is starting. Once you get that out of the way, you'll find the rest of the journey much easier.' – Sinek, 2014

How often do we, as educators, lament the challenges of an overcrowded curriculum? We resonate with phrases like 'There's simply too much', or 'I can't possibly cover it all'. Some of us even resort to turbo-teaching – teach, assess, move on, teach, assess, move on – leaving little room for dialogue or interactive activities. The saddest refrain? 'I don't have time; we just have to get through it.'

In my many years working across a diverse range of schools, I've encountered these plaintive words week after week. Teachers make these comments because they care deeply about the academic success and well-being of their students but also feel compelled to cover everything in the mandated curriculum. Believe me, I bear no judgment. The pressure and resulting anxiety are palpable. Yet, the crux lies not merely in acknowledging this perpetual dilemma but in devising solutions.

Yes, we've witnessed curriculum reviews, each promising streamlined content. However, those tasked with teaching the curriculum remain frustrated, scratching their heads. What has truly changed? How, once again, are they meant to teach it? Not just cover it but inspire student interest and foster genuine learning.

What we need is to work together to create a curriculum that is ready for learning, ready for teachers to teach it and for students to learn it. We're not merely covering content but rather prioritising the most important content so that we have time to make meaningful connections to improve retention and mastery. Most importantly, we are providing our students with the foundations to apply these concepts in new and complex situations.

To address the issue of an overcrowded curriculum, Dr Robert J. Marzano recommends the development of a guaranteed and viable curriculum. He identifies it as the variable most strongly related to student achievement at the school level (Marzano, 2003). Over many years, across many contexts, I have worked with teams as they have embarked on the process of determining specific content that they guarantee will be taught across subject areas and year levels. During this time, I have seen where teams struggle, the pitfalls and traps that they encounter and where the prioritisation process can be derailed. This book tackles various challenges and offers practical solutions, so teams are empowered to utilise one of the most powerful things they can do to improve student achievement.

I have used the term 'a learning-ready curriculum' deliberately to avoid the uncertainty or reluctance that can come from the word 'guarantee'. As educators we are sometimes hesitant to use the word, often saying that it is hard to really guarantee something. The word doesn't fully capture the purpose of the process. Yes, we are making sure that the same content is being taught in all classes, but it is more than that. It's a process of gaining clarity and agreement about the curriculum expectations, so that we are prepared to teach; we have set priorities, we spend enough time on key concepts and we have designed learning pathways, so students are ready to engage with a curriculum that is learning-ready.

Laying the foundation and establishing the 'Why'

Simon Sinek, an English-born American author best known for his book, *Start with Why*, published in 2009, focuses on the importance of purpose and trust when leading initiatives. He reminds us that 'People don't buy what you do; they buy why you do it' (Sinek, 2009). So, let's establish our why. Why engage in the work of creating a learning-ready curriculum? In doing so, we also answer the question 'If this work is so important, why doesn't _____ do it for us?' Fill in the blank with whatever your state or territory curriculum authority is called, your system organisation, your curriculum co-ordinator – basically anyone else but me. The underlying question remains the same, 'Why do I, as a busy teacher, need to do this?'

The first 'why' relates to the nature of the curriculum itself and the disparities we encounter between the intended curriculum, the implemented curriculum and then, of course, what students really learn. Research indicates that there can be considerable differences between all three and it is these gaps that we need to resolve due to the ongoing repercussions for the students we serve (Marzano 2003).

The intended curriculum refers to the curriculum that is designed and communicated within curriculum frameworks and other formal documents. It is what is expected to be taught and learned. The implemented curriculum, on the other hand, is the curriculum that is taught in the classroom. It is the curriculum teachers put into action daily and students engage with, the curriculum that is taught when the classroom door is closed.

So why are there gaps? There are various factors to consider, with the most prominent factor being how the statements in the curriculum are interpreted, especially with a standard referenced curriculum document where the statements are often broad and unclear.

Curriculum standards are statements of what students need to demonstrate at key learning junctures in a particular learning area or subject. They provide a fixed reference point and common language that teachers can use to describe student achievement. They are not a description of what is meant to be taught. In Australia, the standards are accompanied by content descriptions which outline what teachers are expected to teach and students are expected to learn to master the requirements of the achievement standard. Content elaborations are provided as optional resources supporting teachers with suggestions about how they might teach the content.

Although content descriptions and elaborations inform an understanding of the achievement standard, the standards are still open to multiple interpretations. Sometimes, this is due to the wording within the standard, the different levels of experience within the team or even how literal someone might be interpreting the standard. For example, the mathematics achievement standard for year 3 students in Australia includes the ability to tell time to the nearest minute (ACARA, 2022). This seems straight forward, but there's some ambiguity.

When I was working with a team of year 3 teachers, one of the teachers asked what the standard 'tell time to the nearest minute' meant as we considered the level 3 curriculum standards and subsequent content descriptions. He wanted to know if they had to teach the students to read an analogue clock to the exact minute or if they could round to the nearest five minutes. He pointed out that there was a slight difference between reading digital and analogue clocks. When we read a digital clock, he explained, we usually say the time to the exact minute. But when we read an analogue clock, we often round to the nearest five minutes. The discussion that followed was extremely valuable, as the teachers tried to clarify their own understanding and agree on a common interpretation. Without this important discussion, the teachers in the group might have assessed and reported on slightly different criteria. It is also possible that teachers may have taught slightly different content, with one group teaching the skills of rounding up and rounding down as part of the time telling process, while another group taught counting on and counting back in order to communicate time to the exact minute.

With a clear and shared vision of what the curriculum standards demand and what proficiency looks like, teachers could still focus on some standards more than others. This can cause variations across different year levels in terms of what students have had an opportunity to learn and can lead to potential gaps in student learning if they have missed important content or concepts.

For example, teachers engaging in the prioritisation process once shared with me that they typically didn't spend much time on having students place fractions on a number line, explaining to me that they couldn't see the point of it. And yet, placing fractions on a number line is an important skill for students to learn. It helps them understand the relationship between fractions and whole numbers and provides a visual representation of fractions.

By placing fractions on a number line, students can compare fractions and determine which fraction is greater or less than another fraction. It's an essential skill for students to have as they progress through their years of schooling (Miller & Hudson, 2007). Again, the discussion that followed as teachers in the team talked about why it is an important skill was a great professional learning opportunity for all involved.

Often, by the time we finish engaging in the prioritisation process, I will hear the same teachers who were sceptical about the purpose of the process (sometimes with their arms crossed) say something like 'Wow! I have learned a lot today!'. By this stage their arms are no longer crossed and a furrowed brow has been replaced with a smile. Some even finish by calling it the best professional learning experience they have had. One of the main reasons for this turnaround is that teachers seldom get the time and space to work with their peers to study the intended curriculum. They are often put in a difficult situation and expected to teach without sufficient preparation to do it well.

Sometimes, the prioritisation process highlights areas in which the team itself may realise that they don't have enough understanding of the curriculum expectation or knowledge of the best ways to teach what is required. This is not a problem, but rather a chance for the team to collaborate and seek the information they need – either from someone within the school who knows more or from an outside source. The issue of varying curriculum knowledge is confirmed by the Australian Teacher Workforce Data (ATWA).

The teacher workforce data in the ATWD primarily comes from annual data collected as part of the ATWD Teacher Survey and the data on all registered teachers in each state and territory provided by Teacher Regulatory Authorities. In 2020, at least one-in-four (24%) classroom teachers who taught subjects in each key learning area were teaching out-of-field (AITSL, 2023). 'Teaching out-of-field' is a phenomenon where teachers are assigned to teach subjects or year levels for which they have inadequate training and qualifications (Hobbs & Porsch, 2021). It occurs, for example, when a teacher with a major in mathematics and a minor in science is asked to teach Information Communication Technology. Or when a primary school qualified teacher is asked to teach Early Childhood classes. In Australia, the extent of out-of-field teaching varies across subjects, with the rates for some subject areas being higher than others. In 2020, teachers of technology were most likely to be teaching out-of-field (44%) (AITSL, 2023). The challenges of teaching out-of-field is multi-faceted and leaves many teachers feeling under-confident.

Less confidence in teaching may also occur when new elements or requirements are added to the curriculum. For example, the updated history curriculum requires the teaching of Australia's shared history. This involves the teaching of analysis and the incorporation and understanding of Indigenous perspectives. Meaning, it requires a more balanced understanding of what has occurred in Australia's past, to move forward as a nation and to teach for reconciliation (Papadopoulos, 2022). This inclusion may require teams to do further study and investigation.

Another 'why' for establishing clarity and consistency of understanding amongst teachers regarding curriculum expectations relates to our legislative requirements. The Australian Education Act 2013 (the Act) is a federal legislation that regulates the Australian education system. The Act aims to ensure that all Australian students have access to quality education and achieve educational outcomes that contribute to the social and economic development of the nation (Australian Education Act, 2013, s. 3). Regulation 59 of the Act (2013) states that:

For a student who is in any of years 1 to 10, the report must:

(a) give an accurate and objective assessment of the student's progress and achievement, including an assessment of the student's achievement:

    i. against any available national standards.

    ii. relative to the performance of the student's peer group; and

    iii. reported as A, B, C, D or E (or on an equivalent 5-point scale) for each subject studied, clearly defined against specific learning standards; or

(b) contain the information that the Minister determines is equivalent to the information in paragraph (a).

The Act implies that we need clear and consistent understanding of the standards to assess and report accurately.

As we assess student progress and achievement, we need to continually refer to the achievement standards articulated in mandated state and national curriculum documents. This process is referred to as a standard-referenced system. In Australia, we use standard-reference reporting where the focus is on whether an individual meets specific performance expectations. Previously, the more traditional norm-referenced reporting system was utilised by teachers to report progress. Under this system, the focus is on how an individual's performance compares to the average performance of other students. Student achievement is compared to the 'norm' or typical performance of a similar group. The problem with norm reference reporting is that the 'norm' can become what we would typically expect from students at particular year levels. For example, a primary school teacher may have a preconceived notion of the writing skills a typical year 2 student should be able to demonstrate. The teacher then reports on a student's progress compared to this ideal, determining whether the student is demonstrating skills at the same level or performing above or below the skill level expected of a typical year 2 student. Reporting achievement in this way is a slippery slope because the expectation can then vary depending on the teachers' experiences and the 'norm' that they have formed based on their own experience. When we refer to the set standard, we use a shared language to describe achievement and a shared understanding of what that means. When done collaboratively, this creates consistency and clarity of expectations.

It should also be emphasised that we assess and report on the curriculum standard rather than every individual content description within the curriculum documents. This is welcome news for teaching teams who often think that they must assess and report on everything. Remember, the role of the content description is to inform understanding of the standard. They are not for assessment and reporting.

Let's now turn our attention to the students. Is the curriculum ready for our students? Are we ready to communicate the learning expectations to our students so that they have a clear understanding of what is expected and where they are heading?

In 1968, Mary Alice White published an article titled 'The view from the student's desk' and in the article, the late American psychologist, academic and author compared the experience of a student to that of a sailor.

> ... on a ship sailing across an unknown sea to an unknown destination. An adult would be desperate to know where he is going. But a child only knows he is going to school ... The chart is neither available nor understandable to him ... Very

> *quickly, the daily life on board the ship becomes all important … The daily chores, the demands, the inspections become the reality, not the voyage, nor the destination.*

Although written in 1968, White's point still resonates. Student behaviour and engagement in class are some of the major concerns for Australian teachers and education experts. A 2023 Organisation for Economic Co-operation and Development (OECD) report shows that Australian classrooms are among the OECD's most chaotic. This includes minor behaviours like chatting, not following instructions, through to the destruction of property and physical and verbal aggression.

A 2017 study from the Grattan institute (Engaging students: creating classrooms that improve learning) demonstrates that as many as 40% of Australian students are unproductive at any given time in Australian classrooms. Of this 40%, up to 20% of students are passively disengaged. This affects student learning and increases teachers' stress level.

Students disengage when they don't understand the goal or purpose of what they are being asked to do. Over the past ten years, research on goal setting has shown many advantages (The Conversation, 2021) including improved engagement, learning and achievement. But if we, as a team, aren't clear on what the curriculum expectations are, how can we convey clear learning goals to our students in a way that demonstrates relevance and purpose?

Another issue we need to bear in mind is our students' readiness level – what do they already know and can do in relation to the curriculum standard? Are they already proficient with the standard? Do they require further enrichment or extension? Or do they have gaps in their learning that need to be remediated to access the current level of learning? Yet another reason for designing a curriculum that is learning-ready – ready for teachers to teach it and for students to learn it.

However, the 'why' without the 'how' has little probability of success (Sinek, 2009). To design a learning-ready curriculum, there are four essential steps:

i. prioritisation of the content for learning

ii. identification of the skills, knowledge and dispositions for the prioritised content

iii. establishment of the most essential prerequisite knowledge

iv. creation of ways to share the learning pathway with students

Those of you familiar with *Collaborative Teams That Work* written by my colleagues, Colin Sloper and Gavin Grift (2020), will notice the alignment between these steps and the tasks required of teams as they map the learning pathway for a cycle of learning. Like them, I have used the term cycle of learning throughout this book. As Colin and Gavin point out, schools refer to the lessons they deliver in different ways, including unit of study, unit of work and teaching program. The use of the term cycle of learning is a deliberate reference to a unit of instruction that focuses on a particular sequence of teaching, usually focused on delivering the skills, knowledge or dispositions related to a prioritised standard or standards. The term also serves to remind teaching teams that the outcome of the cycle is LEARNING – for students and for us as educators (Sloper and Grift, 2020). After all, 'Learning is the Work' (Fullan, 2011).

Chapter 1

PRIORITISATION PROCESS

'Learning is the Work.' – Fullan, 2011

To create a learning-ready curriculum, we first begin by prioritising the standards and content that will be the focus for student learning. Prioritising standards is about determining which standards need more time and focus for students to develop a level of proficiency in. Then devoting most of our instructional time to concentrating on this essential knowledge and skills with supplemental content being woven into or taught separately but with less emphasis.

It is not about eliminating content. Rather, it is about recognising that not all standards are equal. Some standards can be attained quickly, such as understanding the concept of likely and unlikely in mathematics, while concepts associated with place value take more time to master. Other standards can be taught alongside other content. For example, a primary school teacher could teach the concept of tessellation from the mathematics curriculum within an Art unit. Sloper and Grift (2020) suggest that schools and each team of teachers should be clear on what skills, knowledge and dispositions are most important for their students to master for each curriculum level and subject. Without this clarity, teams struggle to design learning experiences that focus on the essential aspects required for each cycle of learning.

While this step can be undertaken by individual collaborative teaching teams within a school, the process is far more effective when it is part of the whole school's strategic focus. The curriculum needs to be aligned across the school for it to be successful and to ensure that gaps and overlaps in the content taught are not created. This approach provides valuable opportunities for the educators within the school to learn from each other as they strengthen their curriculum knowledge. It is an essential process that provides the opportunity to collaboratively agree upon the prioritised content at a deeper level, without taking seductive shortcuts as listed below.

Seductive shortcuts

■ **Copying documents from another school** – this might seem like a quick and easy way to get the job done, but it will not pay off in the long run. By using another school's documents, teams miss out on the valuable discussions that help them develop a shared understanding and agreement of the content that matters most. Nor have they made a commitment to teach the standards and content that they, as a school, deem important.

■ **Outsourcing the process** – assigning the task to one group of curriculum leaders or enthusiastic teachers is tempting, but all educators at a school must be involved to ensure the success of the process. 'High levels of learning for all students can't be achieved unless there are corresponding high levels of learning for all educators' (Sloper & Grift, 2020, p. 19).

■ **Using regular team time** – prioritisation takes time. Time needs to be allocated that is separate from the scheduled time in which teams usually meet. The work involved in prioritisation is best undertaken over a series of staff meetings or during a designated professional learning day so that there is enough time for meaningful conversations and debate.

■ **Viewing prioritisation as a 'one-off'** – this step is an ongoing process requiring refinement. Teams provide feedback while they work with the documents as circumstances within the school change or as content is adjusted within state and national curriculum documents.

■ **Not communicating the purpose clearly** – remember the importance of 'why'. Make sure to spend time at the beginning to communicate to all stakeholders why this work is important, how it will impact on student achievement and support teachers. Ensure clarity and understanding of the key messages and repeat them often. Remember the Rule of Three – 'Tell them what you're going to tell them, tell them, then tell them what you told them'.

Key Points:

- The process of prioritisation is not elimination.
- Prioritisation creates a focused and agreed upon curriculum that is ready for students to learn and for teachers to identify potential gaps in their knowledge of the standard and how to teach it.
- It is not a choose-your-own-adventure. There is a clear process that will be undertaken and criteria to determine the priority standards and content.

Prioritisation steps

1. Clarify terminology

As a leader, it is important to clarify the language you will consistently use in your school. You need language to describe the standards that will be continually referenced and assessed. For example, in terms of prioritised standards/content, I often refer to this as prioritised standards though there have been other alternatives such as power standards (Ainsworth, 2003), learning targets (Moss & Brookhart, 2012) or essential learnings (Wiggins & McTighe, 2005). Whichever you choose, share it and use it consistently. Do not underestimate this step. If we continually interchange the curriculum and assessment language that we use, teachers, parents and students may perceive changes to the content or processes when there are none (Heflebower, 2020).

2. Be prepared

Value the process. Determine a suitable location and ensure that the necessary materials are available for all participants to engage fully in the discussions. This includes copies of the curriculum documents, highlighters, sticky notes, chart paper and markers, etc. Although the process can be documented electronically, my experience has been that paper copies are extremely useful because they can be viewed by everyone, plus it is easy for teachers to highlight and add comments. It can be useful to have the template in Appendix A, enlarged as A3 copies.

3. Establish norms

Norms are rules or principles that define how the group members will interact, communicate and work together. They can help prevent or resolve conflicts, ensure all voices are heard and create a positive and productive environment for collaborative decision making. Remember that norms are best co-constructed by the group. Here are a few examples below that you might consider. They have been divided into communication and participation. For a more detailed discussion on norms, see *Mastering Meetings That Matter: 8 Essentials for Making Your Meetings More Productive* (Grift, Sloper & De Blasio, 2023).

Sample norms

Communication

- Listen actively and attentively to others.
- Share relevant accurate information and opinions.
- Ask clarifying and probing questions.
- Avoid interrupting, dominating or dismissing others.
- Seek to understand different perspectives and experiences.
- Acknowledge and appreciate the contributions of others.

Participation

- Engage fully and actively in the process.
- Contribute your ideas, skills and expertise.
- Invite and encourage the participation of others.
- Respect the diversity of each group member.
- Value the collective wisdom of the group.

In my experience and that of my colleagues, teams will sometimes resist establishing norms with statements such as 'we're all really nice people, we don't need norms', 'we all get along really well, we don't need norms' or even, 'we're adults, not kids, we don't need norms'. Whilst these statements may be true, they miss the point as to why norms are an important element of prioritisation. If resistance occurs, hold your ground, support the teams in the establishment of their operating norms and reiterate again why the norms are so important.

Norms help ensure that time available is not wasted as a team engages in conversations that are designed to increase student and teacher learning. The norms may create a collaborative environment where staff learn how to set aside unproductive patterns of listening, responding and inquiring, or learn how to aim for consensus when it comes to the decision-making processes needed to prioritise the standards and content (Tamblyn et al., 2023).

4. Consensus building

Consensus building is a decision-making process that is more effective than simple voting because it results in all team members 'consenting' to the prioritisation decisions. It means arriving at a decision that each member of the group can accept and support. It may not be everyone's first choice in terms of what is prioritised. It may not even be anyone's first choice, but it's a decision everyone can live with (Heflebow, Heogh & Warrick, 2021). Attention to consensus means that everyone understands the why behind the decisions.

5. Select the content area focus

Due to time constraints, schools sometimes decide to focus the prioritisation process on one content area of the curriculum. For example, a whole-school approach in a primary school may initially focus on the number and algebra strands in mathematics or the reading standards in English before moving on to consider the measurement in mathematics or speaking and listening standards in English.

6. Match the standards and content descriptions

In the Australian curriculum documents, the standards are written as a paragraph (ACARA, 2022). Separate these into single statements and ensure that there is only one focus for each statement. For example, a year 7 mathematics team may split the standard 'Students use formulas for the areas of triangles and parallelograms and the volumes of rectangular and triangular prisms to solve problems' into two statements:

  i. Students use formulas for the areas of triangles and parallelograms to solve problems.

  and

  ii. Students use formulas for volumes of rectangular and triangular prisms to solve problems.

The next step would normally be to match the curriculum standard with the corresponding content description as they give the teams more clarity around the meaning and expectation of the standard.

Previously, I have found this to be a rich source of discussion and clarification as teachers work together to determine the links. However, this process has become much simpler in Australia with the introduction of Version 9 of the Australian Curriculum in 2022. The link between the achievement standard and the content descriptions have been made clearer through hyperlinks. See Figure 1.1 for an example:

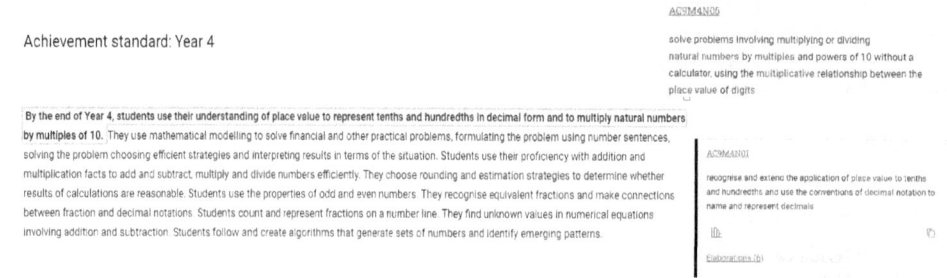

Figure 1.1: Hyperlinks between highlighted achievement standard and content descriptions (ACARA, 2022)

It is still worthwhile having the standard statements and content descriptions for easy reference as the teams progress through their discussions as shown in the example below.

Standard	Content Description
Students use formulas for the areas of triangles and parallelograms to solve problems	solve problems involving the area of triangles and parallelograms using established formulas and appropriate units (AC9M7M01) (ACARA, 2022)
Students use formulas for volumes of rectangular and triangular prisms to solve problems	solve problems involving the volume of right prisms, including rectangular and triangular prisms, using established formulas and appropriate units (AC9M7M02) (ACARA, 2022)

Consider prepopulating the templates with the standard statements and content descriptions. This will save the teams a great deal of time, thus affording them more energy to engage in important discussions regarding prioritisation. In preparation for a recent professional learning day with a school, I did exactly that and it was greatly appreciated by all.

If your state or territory curriculum authority doesn't include the hyperlinks between the achievement standard and content descriptions, consider going to the ACARA site first. Then, cross-check between your state or territory documents and the ACARA documents and adjust where needed. For example, at the time of writing this book, Version 2.0 of the VCAA Mathematics curriculum doesn't include the hyperlinks. However, after cross-checking, there were very few adaptations that needed to be made. One example of an inconsistency was the inclusion of 'investigate number sequences involving multiples of 3, 4, 6, 7, 8 and 9' (VC2M4N02) which wasn't included in the ACARA Level 4 Number and Algebra version.

7. **Focus on the criteria**

Familiarise all teachers with the criteria for determining priority standards/content and the thinking behind each criterion. Without criteria for determining if the content is a priority, there is a risk of teachers picking and choosing aspects of the standards they feel are the highest priority based on gut feel alone, previous experience or comfort levels. The criteria also help to focus the discussion and introduce a shared language. This allows teachers to consider each standard and its matching content descriptions in terms of importance. In the past, the criteria I've used as a starting point were generated by Larry Ainsworth (2003). His criteria were as follows:

Endurance: Standards that focus on knowledge and skills that will be relevant throughout a student's lifetime.

Leverage: Standards that focus on knowledge and skills used in multiple academic disciplines.

Readiness: Standards that focus on knowledge and skills that are necessary for success in the next grade level or course.

However, I have found that teams can sometimes become bogged down with the wording used within the Ainsworth criteria. Also, based on my experience and discussions with colleagues and leaders over many years, there are other criteria to consider in addition to the three listed. I propose the following lenses and guiding questions to consider in the prioritisation process:

Prerequisite knowledge – Is this knowledge or skill students will need for future learning? If they miss this knowledge or skill, will it impact later when more complex concepts are introduced? This is the criterion that most teachers will concentrate on and for good reason.

Longevity – Is this knowledge or skill students will require beyond this cycle of learning, test or unit of work? For example, the ability to summarise is important throughout schooling and across multiple subject areas (it, therefore, has both endurance and leverage which are included in the Ainsworth criteria).

Context – Based on our previous experience and existing data, does this knowledge or skill typically require more or less time to gain proficiency? Or are there pre-existing gaps in learning that will impact students' learning?

For example, a history Head of Department, based on school data, was concerned with the way year 10 students were engaging with methods of research. Student results were typically below what would be expected and the concern was that these research skills were important for students to be successful in senior level units of study. Focusing on communicating to students the importance of research whilst also reviewing research methods became a priority for the team. The decision was also made to review how these skills were being addressed in previous year levels. Questions such as 'Are we communicating the importance of research methods to students?' and 'Are we prioritising research methods across all classes?' became a focus for discussion.

Considering context was very important in a special school where I was guiding teams through the prioritisation steps recently. Due to the learning needs of their students, it was important to be very prudent as they made decisions about which standards and content descriptions were going to be the most important for their students to master. Front and centre in the minds of these incredibly dedicated teachers was the needs of their students, which also linked to the criterion of opportunity.

Opportunity – Will our students be disadvantaged in the future if they don't master this standard or content? For example, it might be prioritised in high-stakes testing or assessment used for instructional decision making. In the special school context described earlier, the conversation was more about future employment opportunities and achievement of a certified course that prepares students for the workforce. Therefore, as the teacher teams considered the mathematics standards and associated content descriptions, they decided to focus their attention on the attainment of number and algebra concepts. Even within these sub-strands, the teachers made more detailed decisions. For example, in Level 3, the achievement standard states that students need to be able to represent unit fractions and their multiples in different ways. Whilst considering the associated content description, teachers decided to prioritise $\frac{1}{2}$, $\frac{1}{3}$, $\frac{1}{4}$ unit fractions but not on $\frac{1}{5}$ and $\frac{1}{10}$ because these fractions were less prevalent in the work environment students would typically enter.

The combination of the four lenses indicates priority standards or content as depicted in Figure 1.2.

Figure 1.2: Four lenses for identifying priority standards

7. Decision making

Keeping in mind the guiding questions – prerequisite knowledge, longevity, context and opportunity (or the criteria used by Larry Ainsworth) – teachers should read through the standards and mark each standard and content description that they feel are the most important. Previously, my colleague Colin Sloper and I have used a template similar to the one below for this process.

Standard	Content Description	Prerequisite knowledge	Longevity	Context	Opportunity	Priority	Supporting
		Is this knowledge or a skill that students will need for future learning?	Is this knowledge or a skill that students will require beyond this cycle of learning, test or unit of work?	Is this knowledge or a skill that our students typically require more or less time to gain proficiency?	Will our students be disadvantaged in the future if they don't master this standard?		

Table 1.1
Example recording template

This phase should be done independently and should be kept to ten minutes or less. If teachers have too much time, they tend to overthink the process and highlight too much. Next, team members should each share the standards and content descriptions they marked. The groups should discuss the following:

- Where do we agree?
- Where do we disagree?
- Should any of these standards be combined or clustered?

The team should then agree on which standards and content descriptions are most important. Teams usually choose eight to fifteen standards for each subject area and level, but these numbers are not fixed and can vary. Don't rush this stage as the discussion and consensus-forming is a source of professional learning as team members discuss the meaning of the standard and how it meets or doesn't meet the criteria. If it doesn't meet the criteria, the team will mark the standard as a supporting or supplementary standard that will be taught and assessed alongside another standard. Or it may be taught and assessed separately, but with less time spent on it.

Make sure to record the thinking of the group and include any notes that may be important for further discussion.

Below is an example of a partially completed form for Foundation English using the Australian Curriculum v. 9. In this example, the team has identified the achievement standard and then the related content descriptions. They have used the criteria to decide if the achievement standard needs to be prioritised. Sometimes, teams may decide that not all related content descriptions need to be prioritised – they might be taught incidentally alongside other standards and content descriptions. Understanding that words are units of meaning and can be made of more than one meaningful part is a concept that the team discussed as something that they would teach incidentally while students were reading and writing. They also decided that it wouldn't be prioritised for assessment.

You can see from the example that the team has colour-coded the standards and content descriptions according to their level of priority. The green ones are the essential standards that will be the main focus of teaching and assessment. The yellow ones are supporting content that will be taught in connection with the prioritised standards. The team has also added some notes to explain their rationale for their choices. They may also highlight any connections or gaps between the standards and content descriptions. This process helps the team to clarify their understanding of the curriculum and to plan their instruction and assessment accordingly.

Standard	Content Description	Prerequisite knowledge	Longevity	Context	Opportunity	Priority	Supporting
		Is this knowledge or a skill that students will need for future learning?	Is this knowledge or a skill that students will require beyond this cycle of learning, test or unit of work?	Is this knowledge or a skill that our students typically require more or less time to gain proficiency?	Will our students be disadvantaged in the future if they don't master this standard?		
Students read words including consonant–vowel–consonant words and some high-frequency words.	**Read and write some high-frequency words and other familiar words** **AC9EFLY14** *Understand that words are units of meaning and can be made of more than one meaningful part* AC9EFLY15					YES	AC9EFLY15 to be taught incidentally throughout all units of study.

Table 1.2: Completed example: Foundation English

8. Vertical alignment

Once consensus is formed, teams should collate their final responses and begin to consider how concepts are developed across year levels. The vertical alignment process ensures that unintended gaps are not created. Depending on time constraints, vertical alignment might take place at a later date.

Useful suggestions to aid this step are as follows:

- Have the standard statements and associated content descriptions listed on chart paper for each level or use an enlarged version of the template from Table 1.2.

- Display the completed charts or templates on the wall to make it easier for viewing.

- Assign teams to consider the responses from the level above and below the level they focused on initially. For example, a team focused on year 7 science would examine levels 6 and 8 in comparison with the content they decided to prioritise for year 7.

- Identify and record any places where there are gaps, repetitions or omissions. A gap is when there are standards that should be taught in more than one level and are missing from a particular level. Redundancies occur when there are overlapping standards that don't need to be taught in more than one level. Lastly, omissions are when there are standards likely to be included on state or national assessments and they are completely missing from two or more levels.

- Leave the documents up on a wall in the staff room or central location for a little while for people to add additional comments or observations.

To aid in conversation, the following questions were suggested by Tammy Heflebower and her colleagues (2014):

- Are there year levels where there are gaps in learning? Are there standards that should be taught in more than one level which are missing from certain levels or have been given less priority? (Gaps)

- Are there instances where the standards are taught more than once in a level or taught in previous levels? (Redundancies)

- Are there levels where important standards have been overlooked? (Omissions)

Once any necessary amendments have been made, teams should then go back and revise the charts to reflect the decisions made during the discussion.

9. Sequence and pace

The next task for teams is to sequence the teaching of the standards and identify which time period they will be taught. For example, teachers in Victoria decided to teach 'compare and order two collections according to their quantity' (VCMNA038). They did so by demonstrating 'adding one more to' and 'taking one away from' in practical and everyday situations (VCMNA039), then identifying groups as being 'one', 'more' or 'less' (VCMNA037) in sequence during the first term of the school year, revising throughout the year.

Teams may also show how certain standards might be clustered and taught within one cycle of learning or focus of study. For some learning areas, the pacing may span two years. As can be seen in year 7 and 8 Design Technologies where the achievement standard to be demonstrated by the end of year 8 is 'students develop and modify creative digital solutions, decompose real-world problems and evaluate alternative solutions against user stories and design criteria'. A team may make the decision to focus on developing and modifying creative digital solutions and decomposing real-world problems in year 7 and then evaluating alternative solutions against user stories and design criteria in year 8.

10. Continue to monitor

It is important to continue to monitor the viability of the document. Remember that the final document of prioritised standards and their pacing is not static. Do adjustments need to be made? Can it realistically be taught in the instructional time available? To answer these questions, leaders need to solicit feedback from colleagues about the effectiveness and relevance of the document. Based on available data and feedback, the document may need to be revised to better align with the needs of students as well as state and national requirements. This is an ongoing process of reflection and improvement that ensures the quality and rigour of the prioritisation process.

A school I worked with in Queensland was showcased as having one of the best curriculum documentations in the state. However, as tempting as it may have been to leave these documents as is, teams revisited the documents each year to consider if any adjustments needed to be made. They usually only needed to make minor tweaks and in doing so created shared ownership and understanding of the documentation as new members joined the teams. It also helped to ensure that the documents were still relevant and viable.

Conclusion

A learning-ready curriculum, like a guaranteed and viable curriculum, is not a proper noun. It is not a concrete object or something that is contained within a booklet or available online. A learning-ready curriculum is the commitment between and among teachers to teach what the team has agreed are the prioritised standards (Texas Elementary Principals & Supervisors Association's TEPSA News, August 2016).

The process of prioritising curriculum standards is not a one-off task, but a continuous cycle of building shared knowledge about what students should know and be able to do. Teams need to collaborate and consult with each other, as well as with other stakeholders, to ensure that the curriculum document reflects the most current and relevant expectations and needs of the students as well as the school community. It's an opportunity for teams to engage in professional dialogue to gain a deeper understanding of the curriculum, taking a further step toward narrowing the gap between the intended and the implemented curriculum.

Final word

DON'T	DO
DON'T complain about too much content to teach.	Prioritise the content to determine where most time needs to be spent for students to learn the important concepts.
DON'T use the term 'cutting' or 'culling' the curriculum.	Use the term 'prioritisation' or determine a focused and agreed curriculum.
DON'T make the process a choose-your-own-adventure.	Work as a team to gain clarity and consistency about priority standards and criteria for decision making.
DON'T shortcut the process or take seductive detours.	Allow time and space for discussions – the end-product is valuable but the discussions that occur along the way are invaluable. Ensure teachers have the materials and resources needed to engage in the process.
DON'T make the document a museum piece.	Continually monitor the viability of the curriculum and review and revise as needed over time.

Planning questions

- Which of the Dos and Don'ts will you be most mindful of as you engage with the prioritisation process?

- Who are the main stakeholders in this process? What will you need to be mindful of as you work with these people?

- What will your key messages be as you speak with these different stakeholders?

- How will teams provide feedback about the process or their professional learning needs?

Chapter 2

IDENTIFY THE SKILLS, KNOWLEDGE AND DIS-POSITIONS FOR THE PRIORITISED STANDARDS

'No one can whistle a symphony. It takes a whole orchestra to play it.' – H.E. Luccock

Once the prioritised standards and content have been identified, the next stage in the process of creating a learning-ready curriculum is by reaching an agreement on the specific skills, knowledge and dispositions students will need to show mastery of the standard. This step, which is based on the prioritisation templates created previously (Table 1.1), is best completed by teams as part of the planning process as they begin to map the learning pathway for a cycle of learning. Rather than relying on their individual interpretation of the curriculum, reaching joint agreement leads to more clarity and consistency.

This stage involves four steps:

1. Unpack the standard
2. Create learning goals
3. Identify professional learning needs
4. Make a commitment

UNPACK THE STANDARD

As previously discussed, standards are typically broad statements and, as such, are open to multiple interpretations. In my experience, it has been common to have several different interpretations of the meaning of a standard within the one group of teachers. It is essential, therefore, that teachers work collaboratively to break down the standard into the specific skills and knowledge that will be the focus of teaching. In other words, they need to be able to clearly articulate an answer to the question 'What do we want all students to know and be able to do as a result of this cycle of learning?'. Furthermore, unclear or poorly worded phrasing can prevent students from clearly understanding what is expected from them (Heflebower, Hoegh and Warrick, 2014).

Without this step, multiple teachers who teach the same standards across the same year level may be teaching slightly different content or have different expectations in terms of what mastery of the standard looks like. When this occurs, subsequent conversations about assessment and reporting are compromised. In contrast, when teachers engage in this process, they ensure consistency and coherence in planning, delivery and assessment across different classes and year levels. It's not that each teacher must teach in the same way, but they do need to commit to teach the same things with the same level of expectations in terms of what mastery looks like.

To develop a common understanding of the standard, teachers need to closely consider the standard statement and supporting resources provided by national or state and territory curriculum authorities. Content descriptions linked to the standard should be analysed and if further clarification is required, teachers may also consider the standard elaborations that are listed under each content description. Keep in mind that the elaborations are optional. They simply provide teachers with suggestions of ways to teach the content descriptions. Work samples provided by ACARA provide further insights into what mastery of the standard looks like. Each collection of work samples shows evidence of what students have learned, aligned with aspects of the achievement standards for a subject or learning area.

To illustrate the process, let us consider two examples from different learning areas and curriculum levels that have been identified as priority standards. The first example is from English, year 6. The second example is from Design and Technologies, year 9 and 10.

English, year 6

The achievement standard of focus is:

> *'They explain how language features including literary devices, and visual features influence audiences.'*

Once we look at the content descriptions, the expectation of the standard is obtained.

In this instance, there are twelve content descriptions highlighted on the ACARA website as associated with this standard (https://v9.australiancurriculum.edu.au/f-10-curriculum/learning-areas/english/year-6 – accessed March, 2024).

Where this is the case, a team may decide to focus on three of the content descriptions in a particular cycle of learning. For example,

> - *analyse how text structures and language features work together to meet the purpose of a text, and engage and influence audiences (AC9E6LY03),*
> - *identify authors' use of vivid, emotive vocabulary, such as metaphors, similes, personification, idioms, imagery and hyperbole (AC9E6LA08) and*
> - *identify and explain how images, figures, tables, diagrams, maps and graphs contribute to meaning (AC9E6LA07).*

Although the content descriptions are relatively clear, teams will need to decide on the language features they will focus upon and the types of texts they will explore. Will they focus upon grammar, vocabulary, figurative language, punctuation and images? Will they explore rhetorical devices and figurative language? Or will they decide that in the time available, they need to narrow their focus?

Design and Technologies, year 9 and 10

The achievement standard is:

> *'They explain the contribution of innovation, enterprise skills and emerging technologies to global preferred futures.'*

The associated content description is: analyse the impact of innovation, enterprise and emerging technologies on designed solutions for global preferred futures (AC9TDE10K02) (ACARA, 2022). Teachers need to understand what is meant by emerging technologies and global preferred futures. As stated on the ACARA website, global preferred futures involves students reflecting on how the solutions they design today might be applied in the future. The content elaborations provide options such as students collaborating to design solutions to challenges in the Asia region, or investigating scenarios of how the future may unfold and what opportunities and impacts there may be for society and particular groups in a preferred future, for example, by using forecasting and backcasting techniques.

Translate into learning goals

Once the meaning of the standard has been determined, the team can turn their energies towards developing learning goals or intentions. Whether or not you decide to use the term learning goal, intention or even target doesn't matter. But what does matter is that you agree on one term and use it consistently across the school.

The statements should be clear and specific. John Hattie (2009) found that one of the main factors that separates effective and ineffective teachers is knowing the learning intentions and success criteria for their lessons. As a result, they can continuously check their students' progress toward those expected outcomes. Edwin Locke and Gary Latham (2002) showed the impact of teachers having specific goals with effect sizes from 0.42 to 0.80. An effect size such as this translates to a percentile increase of 16 – 29 points in student achievement.

There is often confusion between goals and activities, so check in to see that all teachers understand the differences. Activities are things students will be asked to complete. They are an essential part of good teaching, but they are not ends in themselves (Marzano, 2009). They constitute how the learning goals are to be accomplished. In contrast, a learning goal is a statement of what students will know (knowledge) or be able to do (skills).

Consider the following two examples put forward by Robert Marzano (2009) to highlight the differences:

1. *Students will compare and describe the slopes of two lines.*

   According to Marzano (2009), this is an activity. Comparing is a complex cognitive behaviour that students must do, but there is no clear goal for what they should learn.

2. *Students will understand the differences and similarities between metamorphic, igneous and sedimentary rock.*

   This is a learning goal. Unlike statement (1), which also involves a comparison, there is a clear outcome regarding student understanding.

Make sure that teams continue to base their learning goals on the priority standards and content instead of historical documents or previous units of work. This way, the learning goals stay not only aligned but current.

It is surprising how often, when I work with school teams, they assure me that their units of work all draw from the standards. But when we examine the standard expectations, they discover that they have included expectations that are not required. They have unintentionally added to an already overcrowded curriculum. One memorable day was with a team of Foundation teachers. They were stressed because they believed they had to teach narrative writing to their students, many of whom were EAL/D (English as an Additional Language or Dialect) learners. When we looked at the Foundation standard, we discovered that the expectation was that students were expected to use familiar words, phrases and images to convey ideas. With a sense of relief the teachers remarked, 'That's great, our students are really good at that!'

As teachers translate the standards into learning goals, ensure that the cognitive demand of the standard is maintained. Cognitive verbs indicate the type of mental processes that students must apply when showing their knowledge, understanding and skills. Consider using a resource such as the suite of cognitive verb resources, including a list of common cognitive verbs and cognitive verb overviews developed by the Queensland Curriculum & Assessment Authority – www.qcaa.qld.edu.au/p-10/aciq/frequently-used-resources/cognitive-verbs.

Below is a primary school reading example where the team was focused on the skill of inferring. In addition to the curriculum documents, they accessed resources within their professional library to gain a deeper understanding of the standard.

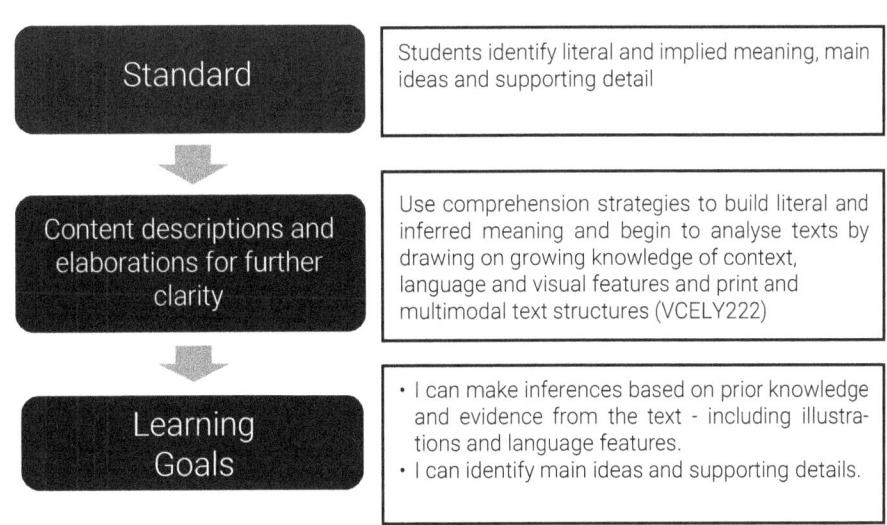

Undertake professional learning

During team conversations, it might reveal that some team members are not sure how to teach the content related to the standard. They might choose to set aside some time for professional reading or ask the leadership team for more professional learning opportunities in this area. Alternatively, they might decide that they have the resources within the group to support one another in professional growth as they continue through the process.

While working with an experienced team of teachers, we started to discuss the year 2 English standard on text comprehension. The teachers realised that they needed to know more about the development of comprehension strategies and if there was a particular sequence that they should use as they introduced the strategies. Fortunately, the school had a good professional library they could access for further research. These resources proved to be incredibly valuable as the team progressed to the next stage in the process to determine the most essential prerequisite knowledge.

When these types of questions arise, and they usually do, it is important to view this as an opportunity for learning rather than a problem with the process itself. It is the reason why it is so important that the teams have strong operating norms in place so that professional trust has been developed and a culture of learning for all has been established.

Commit

Having arrived at the final decisions and reaching a higher level of clarity and shared understanding, each teacher needs to make a commitment to teach these skills, knowledge and dispositions for all students. This commitment ensures that all students, regardless of who their teacher is, receive the same learning opportunities.

Decide how you will monitor that the agreed content is being taught in every classroom. You might consider the following:

- assessment data
- unit plans
- artefacts such as student work samples
- classroom observations

The aim of these monitoring activities is not only to check that the agreed content is followed, but also to help teachers grow professionally and enhance student results.

Conclusion

This chapter has explored how to make a curriculum that is ready for learning by agreeing on the key skills, knowledge and dispositions that students need to achieve the standards. By following this process, teachers can ensure that their curriculum is aligned, coherent and responsive to the needs of all learners. 'Teachers who truly understand what they want their students to accomplish will almost surely be more instructionally successful than teachers whose understanding of hoped-for student accomplishments are murky' (Popham, 2003).

Our next step is to identify the most essential prerequisite knowledge that students need to attain mastery of the priority standards.

Final word

DON'T	DO
DON'T shortcut the process.	Develop a common understanding of the expectations of the standard – what will students need to know and be able to do to demonstrate mastery of the standard?
DON'T use vague and ambiguous wording.	Use language that is clear and specific and, where possible, in language that students can understand.
DON'T dumb down the standard.	Keep the cognitive demand of the standard but adjust the language if needed or pre-teach the vocabulary to ensure student understanding of the goal.
DON'T assume that everyone understands what a learning goal is and how to write one.	Check in to see how teachers are using learning goals and remind them that learning goals are typically overarching statements that develop overtime. They are rarely achieved in a single lesson.
DON'T assume that the intended curriculum is being implemented.	Monitor that the agreed upon content is being taught.

Planning questions

- Which of the Dos and Don'ts will you be most mindful of as you engage with the process of having teachers identify the skills, knowledge and dispositions for the prioritised standards?

- How will teams provide feedback about the process or their professional learning needs?

- What support do you anticipate teams might require?

- In what ways will you monitor that the agreed content is being taught?

Chapter 3

DETERMINE THE MOST ESSENTIAL PREREQUISITE KNOWLEDGE

'You can't build a great building on a weak foundation.' – G. Hinkley

As educators, it is crucial to pinpoint the foundational skills and knowledge necessary for students to achieve mastery of the priority learning goals. Sometimes, this may be content from a previous year level or unit. Because it is important background knowledge, it would be included as a learning target in the learning cycle. Other times, the foundational skills may be a more basic version of the priority standard. Teams will need to reflect on the standard from the previous level and discern the additional skills and knowledge required to meet the new standard. They will then need to consider how they can break down complex concepts into manageable components, ensuring students grasp the fundamental building blocks.

Sloper and Grift (2020) advise that when identifying the prerequisites, teams need to be mindful that they don't have enough time to reteach all the prerequisites, so they should only include the most critical prerequisites. These prerequisites may need a more explicit teaching approach than before to make sure that the students can progress in their learning. If some students didn't learn the prerequisite skills earlier, it is essential that they learn them as fast as possible to enable them to participate in the 'at standard' expectations of the current cycle of learning. 'If we are genuinely trying to close the learning gap, time doesn't allow us the luxury of teaching these skills without a great sense of urgency and priority' (Sloper & Grift, 2020, p. 15).

Let's look at an example used previously to illustrate this point. By the end of year 3, students are expected to be able to tell the time to the nearest minute (ACARA, 2022). When you consider the content descriptions for further clarification, we learn that they need to do this with both analogue and digital clocks using a.m. and p.m. If I am considering the prerequisite knowledge, I would first consider the year 2 standard and then build from there. By the end of year 2, students need to be able to tell time to the hour, half hour, quarter to and quarter past (ACARA, 2022). This is my starting point. But what else do students need to know and be able to do if our focus is on telling time using an analogue clock? Most teachers will identify the following skills as prerequisites:

- counting in fives to 60
- understanding that each segment on the clock represents increments of five minutes
- understanding the role of the hands on the clock
- describing the difference between a.m. and p.m.

From there, I can turn the statements into learning goals, or a sequence of 'I can' statements:

- I can tell the time to the hour, half hour, quarter to and quarter past.
- I can count in fives to 60.
- I can explain that each segment on the clock represents five minutes.
- I can explain the role of the hands on the clock.
- I can describe the difference between a.m. and p.m.

All the skills and understandings identified as foundational knowledge are explicitly within the year 3 units of study for mathematics, thus ensuring alignment between the curriculum and instruction.

When teachers collaborate to identify the prerequisite knowledge, they often realise that in the past, they may have assumed students were already proficient at certain skills. Sometimes, teachers also discover that they may have brushed over certain concepts, forgetting that these sub-skills and simpler concepts were foundational to students' mastery of a skill or knowledge. When we as teachers have expert knowledge of a subject it can be challenging to break down the concepts into their simpler components. For example, referring to the earlier discussed telling time example, year 3 teachers realised that their students didn't really understand that each segment on the clock represented a time period of five minutes. Previously, they had taught students to count in fives to 60 but hadn't really highlighted the minute intervals in between clearly enough. Once they did this, they noticed that most students reached the level of proficiency faster. A teacher of graphics remarked that the process made him really stop to think about what students required and that he, too, in the past, had skipped over skills. In slowing down and breaking the concepts into small, sequential steps, his students were more successful.

Another vital prerequisite is vocabulary. Key terms related to the learning goals need to be identified and explicitly taught. As authors Isabel L. Beck and Margaret G. McKeown (1991) argue, 'research spanning several decades has failed to uncover strong evidence that word meanings are routinely acquired from context' (p. 799). Rather, multiple learning opportunities are required through explicit teaching (Jenkins, Stein & Wysocki,1984). Vocabulary, in particular, academic vocabulary will be discussed further in the next section.

DETERMINE KEY ACADEMIC VOCABULARY

Academic vocabulary refers to the specialised words and terms that are essential for understanding and mastering subject-specific content. In mathematics, this would include words such as equation and expression. In history, words such as federalism and democracy. These terms are often more complex and domain-specific than everyday language.

Researchers Beck, McKeown and Omanson (1987) categorised vocabulary terms into three tiers to help identify words for instruction:

- Tier 1: Basic words used often in everyday conversation (e.g., dog, go, happy, drink). These words typically do not need to be explicitly taught. However, students with learning difficulties or an English as an Additional Language or Dialect background may still benefit from explicit teaching of some tier 1 words.

- Tier 2: More complex, frequently occurring words in academic settings. These are words that are useful across multiple topic and subject areas. (e.g., compare, represent, contrast, collaborate). Students should learn to use tier 2 words in multiple contexts and for multiple purposes.

- Tier 3: Highly specialised words that are related to a specific discipline (e.g., photosynthesis, democracy, algebra). Students should learn to use tier 3 words in the context of the specific subject matter where they are useful.

The combination of tier 3 words and the less-frequent tier 2 words form the basis of academic vocabulary.

Academic vocabulary plays a pivotal role in students' understanding of concepts and, therefore, must be considered as foundation knowledge. It serves as the bedrock of declarative knowledge and acts as an entry point to deeper comprehension. Research has consistently highlighted its significance in overall academic achievement (Baumann & Graves, 2010) since it is closely linked to background knowledge, which is crucial for making connections and inferences (Marzano, 2004). According to Dr Robert J. Marzano, the average correlation between a person's background knowledge of a given topic and the extent to which that person learns new information on that topic is 0.66 (Marzano, 2004). Correlation can tell us whether changes in one variable (e.g., background knowledge) are associated with changes in another variable (e.g., student achievement). A correlation of 0.66 indicates that there is a fairly strong linear relationship between the two variables, meaning that as one variable improves, the other tends to as well. Research has also shown that students' test scores can increase by 33 percentile points when vocabulary instruction focuses on specific words important to the content they are studying (Stahl,1986). This means the difference between achieving 50% or 83% on a test. It could even mean the difference between pass or fail, a C grade or a D.

A whole-school approach is beneficial in identifying key academic vocabulary to ensure consistency and alignment. In a primary school setting, year level teams might identify the key vocabulary, for example, in mathematics and then work together to see where there are omissions or repetition.

In Figure 3.1, you can see that year level teams of teachers from a school in Queensland I was working with initially wrote down the words that they felt were essential. Next, they crossed out those words that had already been identified by previous year level teams. Typically, year level teams will identify approximately 30 words (this number is considered manageable) for each year in the focus subject area. Once the teams checked over the lists and decided that they did not miss important or repeated words, they collated the lists into a final document. See Table 3.1 for an example of the final collated list of words.

Figure 3.1: Example list of words prior to review

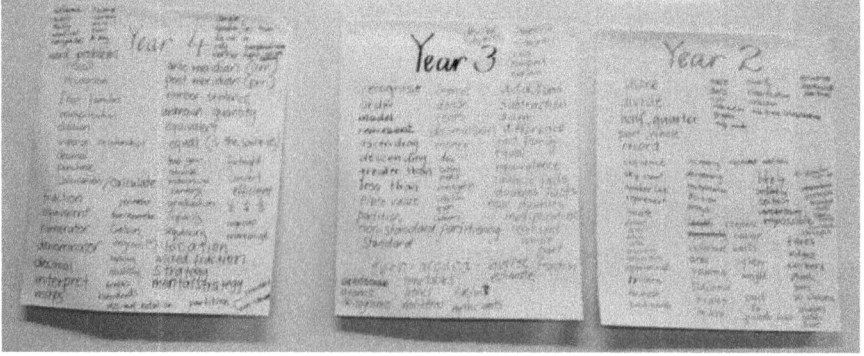

Table 3.1: Final list of collated words from a primary school showing F-3 key terms

FOUNDATION	YEAR 1	YEAR 2	YEAR 3
number	skip count	rearrange	natural numbers
numeral	tens	rename	division
subitise	ones	represent	fraction
partition	order	multiplication	estimate
equal	problems	transaction	reasonable
share	addition	part-whole	number sentence
pattern	subtraction	half	value
repeating	calculate	quarter	rounding
add	strategy	eights	odd
take away	group	increase	even
days of the week	shortest	decrease	property
afternoon	longest	constant	equivalent fractions
morning	compare	analogue	decimal
nighttime	lightest	half hour	number line
volume	heaviest	quarter hour	algorithm
triangle	length	opposite parallel	scale
square	unit	straight	temperature
circle	height	clockwise	angle
rectangle	hours	anticlockwise	grid
2-D	duration	left	axis
curve	month	right	turn
closed	calendar	graph	metric
inside	classify	list	cylinder
underneath	3-D	table	spheres
behind	oval	tally	prism
data	irregular	title	pyramid
object	frequency	direction	faces
measure	record	position	surface
shorter	collect	location	edge
longer	uniform		vertices
	informal		variable

The process is similar for a secondary school where teachers might work in subject area teams to identify approximately 30 words critical to the understanding of the achievement standards for each year level. It's not that other words won't be taught. Rather, this set of essential words will be continually reviewed and revised to ensure that students learn them. If students have not mastered these terms, additional learning experiences should be provided.

Recently, a science teacher shared with me the difference she could see between classes where teachers had or had not fully committed to the process of teaching the identified words. Common summative assessments demonstrated students in classes where teachers adopted the practice outperformed other students where the practice wasn't applied. Reportedly, they were also more confident as they were taking the assessment (test), needing to ask fewer questions of the supervising teachers. This observation coincides with research studies that have shown there is a correlation between academic vocabulary and

- success on test scores,
- level of reading comprehension, irrespective of reading ability,
- speed and accuracy of study behaviour and
- student interest.

We shouldn't think about vocabulary teaching as another thing to do '... the teaching of vocabulary is not a luxury; it is an equity issue' (Berne & Blachowicz, 2008).

In several works (Marzano, 2004, 2020; Marzano & Pickering, 2005), Robert Marzano describes a six-step process that incorporates research-based elements of effective key academic vocabulary instruction. These six steps are as follows:

1) Provide a description, an explanation or an example of the new term.

2) Ask students to restate the description, explanation or example in their own words.

3) Ask students to construct a picture, symbol or graphic representing the term or phrase.

4) Periodically engage students in activities that help them add to their knowledge of the terms to which they have previously been exposed to.

5) Periodically ask students to discuss the terms with one another.

6) Periodically involve students in games that allow them to play with terms.

(Marzano, 2020, p. 38)

Steps 1-3 are used for each word while steps 4-6 are applied to groups of words. Steps 4-6 provide opportunities for students to review and revise what they have learned as a result of the first three steps. Students should experience at least one of these first three steps at least once a week. One word of warning: don't skip step 3.

Creating an image is important for retention and is linked to dual-coding theory. Dual-coding helps students combine information they receive (verbally and visually) in their working memory and store it efficiently in long-term memory. This reduces cognitive load, allowing students to quickly retrieve knowledge when they face more challenging tasks or apply information to new situations.

See Appendix B for an overview of the key steps for teachers.

Create pre-assessments and establish readiness levels

Determining the most essential prerequisite knowledge and skills creates a valuable blueprint for assessment and differentiation as teams consider what students might already know and be able to do to establish student readiness levels. We know from extensive research in the area of educational psychology that if tasks are too demanding for students, or if they provide little to no challenge, engagement and consequently academic achievement are hindered (Vygotsky, 1978). Consequently, it is vital that before embarking on a learning cycle or unit of study, we need to conduct some form of pre-assessment to gauge students' existing knowledge and readiness. Readiness here refers to a student's entry point – how ready a student is to learn a particular concept, skill or content in the lesson or unit (Porta, 2024). Without such information, a teacher will deliver the same content in the same way to the whole class with no differentiation (Sloper & Grift, 2020).

There can be a reluctance to pre-assess students with a belief that it detracts from valuable instructional time. However, in the end, it saves time as it clearly identifies where students might already have a firm understanding of the content and might simply need a quick revision before moving on or identify gaps in understanding that need to be addressed prior to teaching, thus saving the time of having to reteach because students were not ready to grasp new content. The best analogy I have seen and used to highlight this practice is fast-forward, pause, play and rewind buttons.

Based on pre-assessment data:

- Do we need to rewind because students don't have the foundational knowledge required? Perhaps we might even need to go back further.
- Do students have prior knowledge of the topic because it has been covered in previous year levels and, therefore, we can move forward or even fast-forward?

The most important button of course is the pause button. It is essential that we leave enough time between the pre-assessment and beginning to teach so we can analyse the data and adjust plans as required. Sadly, a far too common practice is to pre-assess and then teach the unit of work as already planned. This is a waste of time and energy for all concerned.

It is important to remember that a pre-assessment does not have to be an onerous, time-consuming task. It could be as simple as any of the following:

- exit/entry tickets – see Appendix C for examples. These can easily be recreated in digital form instead of the traditional paper format.
- hand signals – fist to five for example where the fist shows I have no understanding through to five fingers indicating a high level of confidence.
- KWL charts (know, want to know and already learned)
- quizzes such as Kahoot or Quizizz (which will even create the quiz questions for you using AI)
- surveys
- mini whiteboards
- empty outlines for students to complete
- diagrams and graphic organisers – for example, the double bubble map such as shown below comparing expressions and equations.

Figure 3.2: Completed double bubble map

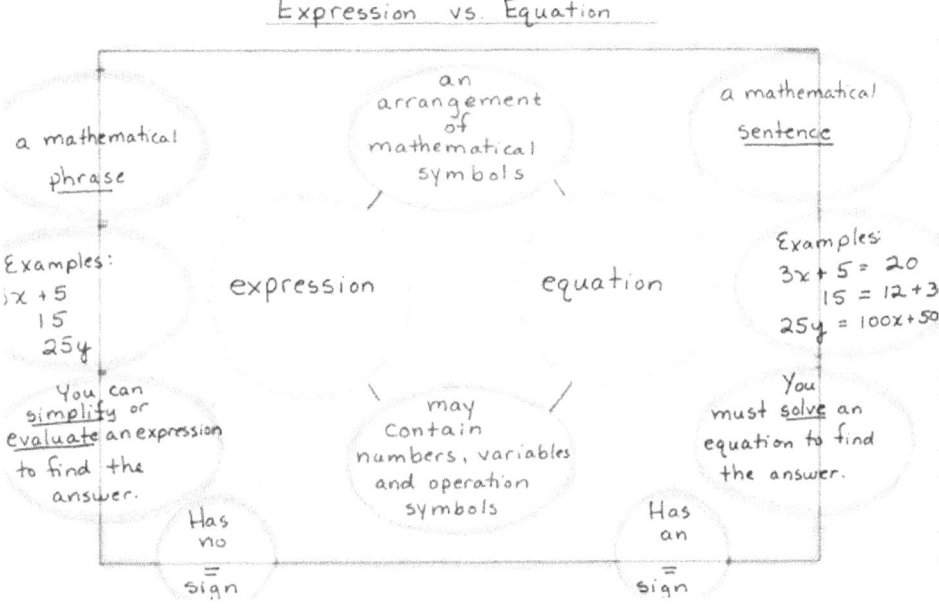

These pre-assessment techniques can be used on an on-going basis to gather evidence of student learning to inform next steps for instruction and differentiation.

Consider enrichment and extension approaches

Additionally, pre-assessment data can reveal that some students may already have mastery of the identified knowledge and skills. These students will require either enrichment, extension or a combination of the two to foster academic growth as well as social and emotional well-being.

Colin Sloper and Gavin Grift (2020) define enrichment as having students who are already proficient apply the target skills and knowledge in some way to encourage deeper exploration. This may include higher-order questions, advanced readings or real-world applications, including project-based learning approaches.

Some examples of enrichment activities are:

- ■ Asking students to create a product, such as a poster, a brochure, a podcast or a video, that demonstrates their understanding of the topic and conveys it to a specific audience.

- Asking students to conduct a research project on a related topic of their interest, using various sources of information and following the steps of inquiry.

- Asking students to design and implement a service-learning project that addresses a real-world problem or need in their community, using the skills and knowledge they have learned.

- Asking students to analyse and evaluate different perspectives, arguments or evidence on a controversial issue or a complex problem.

For this process, teams often find it helpful to utilise lists of cognitive verbs and phrases from the New Taxonomy of Educational Objectives created by Marzano and Kendall (2007). Webb's Depth of Knowledge wheel is also useful. When utilising these resources, teams will consider the level of complexity of the target standard and then create a task at a higher level.

Let's consider an example using the Marzano and Kendall taxonomy depicted in Table 3.2.

Table 3.2: Marzano and Kendall's New Taxonomy

Level of Difficulty	Mental Processes	Example Terms and Phrases
Level 4: Knowledge Utilisation – Applying information or processes in order to complete a larger task	Decision Making	Decide Select the best among the following alternatives Which of these is most suitable
	Problem Solving	Solve How would you overcome Develop a strategy to
	Experimenting	Generate and test What would happen if How would you determine if
	Investigating	Research Take a position on How/why did this happen

Level 3: Analysis – Extending or elaborating on knowledge in a reasoned manner	Matching	Categorise Compare and contrast Create an analogy or metaphor
	Classifying	Organise Sort Identify categories
	Analysing Errors	Identify errors in reasoning Identify problems Identify misunderstandings
	Generalising	What conclusions can be drawn What inferences can be made Form conclusions
	Specifying	Make and defend Predict Deduce
Level 2: Comprehension – Understanding and interpreting knowledge such that it can be stored in long-term memory	Integrating	Describe how or why Describe the relationship between Summarise
	Symbolising	Depict Represent Illustrate
Level 1: Retrieval – Bringing stored information from long-term memory to working memory	Recognising	Recognise (from a list) Select (from a list) Identify (from a list)
	Recalling	Name List Identify who, where, when
	Executing	Use Demonstrate Make

Source: Marzano et. al., 2016

If the cognitive demand of the target is to 'describe how or why', which is at the comprehension level of the Marzano and Kendall taxonomy, a higher-level task for enrichment may involve students engaging in a task requiring analysis such as identifying misunderstandings in an argument or comparing and contrasting to show the similarities and differences between two entities. The highest cognitive level in the Marzano and Kendall taxonomy is knowledge application which involves decision making, problem solving, experimenting and investigating. Students might be asked to select the best option between several alternatives or generate and test a hypothesis, thus, prompting the student to go beyond the cognitive level of difficulty of the original target standard.

Extension, on the other hand, means the 'considered action of moving the proficient student to a higher level of skills and knowledge, which is often drawn from the curriculum for the following year or level' (Sloper & Grift, 2020). This, of course, requires careful planning and collaboration among teachers, students and caregivers, as well as ongoing assessment and feedback because it will have implications for future years. It is also essential to ensure that the student has a deep understanding of the content rather than a superficial, surface level understanding.

Conclusion

Thus far, we have identified the most essential knowledge and skills and determined the prerequisites necessary for students to meet the prioritised standards and content. These prerequisites serve as foundational building blocks. We have also considered what enrichment or extension might look like for students who are already demonstrating proficiency of the targeted standards and content.

This has resulted in three distinct levels of achievement:

- Prerequisite level: fundamental concepts and skills including vocabulary
- At standard level: the expected standard and demonstration of proficiency in the core content
- Enrichment level: opportunities to broaden and deepen student understanding

In the beginning, this process may seem cumbersome, but like any type of procedural knowledge, the more often teacher teams engage in the process, the more fluent and confident they will become.

Now, our focus shifts to communicating this pathway to our students. By clearly outlining how each level connects to the next, we empower students to understand their journey toward mastery.

Final word

DON'T	DO
DON'T assume students already know all the terms you will be using.	As a team, determine the key vocabulary words that will be a focus and explicitly teach them.
DON'T use a pre-assessment and then teach the same unit regardless of the data.	Use the pre-assessment information to determine the readiness of students and adjust the plan as needed.
DON'T begin teaching on 'day one'.	Build time into the plan to allow for the analysis and actioning of data.
DON'T wait until the end of the unit or cycle of learning to assess student learning.	Use on-going formative assessment to inform the next steps for instruction and monitor student learning.
DON'T forget about the students who are already proficient at the standard.	Build in enrichment or extension approaches as needed for individual students.

Planning questions

- How will students record key academic vocabulary and important tier 2 words (e.g., cognitive verbs)? Will they use a vocabulary notebook or record words in a digital format?

- What processes will you use for teams to create vertical alignment of key vocabulary terms to reduce replication or omissions?

- In what ways might you monitor that key vocabulary is being taught? Will you conduct walkthroughs and observations?

- As you encourage the use of pre-assessment data, what might you need to be mindful of as you work with staff? What might be some of the potential challenges?

Chapter 4

DISCUSS WAYS OF SHARING THE LEARNING PATHWAY WITH STUDENTS

'Wisdom is not a product of schooling but of the lifelong attempt to acquire it' – Albert Einstein

The final step in building a learning-ready curriculum is where the rubber really hits the road as we create a transparent learning pathway for our students to foster motivation, self-awareness and a sense of purpose. When students know the specific goal of each lesson and how it fits into the bigger learning sequence, they can see how the skills and knowledge they learn are relevant (Sloper & Grift, 2020).

Much of the work for this step has already been completed. Now, we simply need to ensure that what has been created is articulated in student-friendly language and presented in such a way that students are able to see the incremental gains required to acquire mastery of the prioritised standards or content. This process supports the development of metacognition and self-regulatory behaviours, skills that are vital for academic success and for life.

Metacognition and self-regulatory behaviours

Metacognition is often referred to as thinking about one's own thinking. Although this common description reflects the literal translation, cognition about cognition, originally referred to by American developmental psychologist John Flavell in the mid-1970s, is so much more. Metacognition involves being aware of our cognitive processes, monitoring our learning and adjusting as needed.

John Flavell and Ann Brown defined metacognition as knowledge about cognition and regulation of cognition (Baker, 2010). Both require self-reflection as I consider my thinking processes and progress towards a set goal or the completion of a task. Metacognitive knowledge incorporates:

- Knowledge of the task at hand and being able to identify the steps needed. It's about knowing what you know, don't know and need to know.

- Knowledge of strategies and understanding the approaches that could be used to achieve the identified goal or solve the problem.

- Knowledge of self by understanding your own strengths and weaknesses and even the thinking that might get in the way of your learning. For example, automatically giving up and becoming overwhelmed when presented with a difficult task.

Metacognitive regulation is concerned with planning – identifying the problem, choosing a strategy, organising thoughts and anticipating an outcome. Since metacognition is goal-oriented, it is also concerned with monitoring and evaluating – monitoring my efforts while I am working and learning and evaluating the effectiveness of my strategies. Are the strategies working or do I need to choose another approach? Finally, I then evaluate, checking the outcome. How am I doing? Have I reached the goal?

Metacognitive knowledge and regulation are symbiotic. As I evaluate my strategies and approaches, my metacognitive knowledge develops further.

Metacognition is developmental, beginning at an early age and maturing over time (Walsh & Sattes, 2012). Usually, 'inner language', which is needed for metacognition, starts around age five and the more formal thinking processes of metacognition start around age eleven (Costa, 2001). Some students, particularly high-achieving students, have high levels of metacognitive knowledge and regulation but typically these skills need to be explicitly taught (Sternberg, Jarvin, & Grigorenko, 2011; Baker, 2010).

Metacognition also involves self-regulation of our cognitive efforts. This regulation is guided by goals and the steps to achieve them, whether the goal is to keep the current efforts the same or to change it (Carver, Scheier & Fulford, 2008). In an educational context, self-regulation refers to the degree in which students are actively involved in their own learning process (Risemberg & Zimmerman, 1992). In other words, it is the extent to which they participate in setting learning goals and the control they exercise to achieve the goals (Schunk, 2001). Self-regulation can be learned through modelling, scaffolding and direct instruction (Watson, 2004).

Table 4.1 provides an overview of behaviours associated with self-regulation. These behaviours can form the basis for students to self-reflect using prompts such as those in Table 4.2.

Figure 4.1 shows the self-regulating behaviours as a set of prompts for self-reflection. Teachers sometimes incorporate one or two of these focused behaviours into exit strategies such as those included in Appendix C. A teacher I was coaching used similar reflections for students to reflect on their level of commitment and engagement during class. The teacher then collated the results and provided students with a visual graphic of the class results that was tracked over time and compared with individual responses *(Figure 4.1)*.

Self-regulating learning behaviours
Metacognitive planning
Plan: Set goals, organise tasks and create strategies.
Monitor: Consider their progress and adjust strategies as needed.
Reflect: Assess how well they did in relation to their initial goals.
Motivation
Set intrinsic goals: Seek mastery and personal growth.
Persist: Overcome challenges and setbacks.
Value learning: Understand the importance of learning beyond external rewards.
Maintain engagement
Manage time: Allocate time effectively for learning tasks and avoid distractions.
Avoid procrastination: Prioritise tasks and avoid distractions.
Engage: Stay committed to learning activities.
Monitor performance
Adjust strategies: Modify approaches based on task requirements.
Seek help: Know when to seek assistance.
Learn from feedback: Seek and use feedback constructively from different sources, such as teachers, peers and self-assessment.
Self-reflect
Understand themselves: Understand their strengths and weaknesses as a learner.
Attribute success to effort: Understand that effort leads to improvement.
Persist despite difficulties: View challenges as opportunities for growth.

Table 4.1: Self-regulating learning behaviours

Self-regulating learning behaviours	Colour the stars to indicate the how true the statement is for you
1. I plan and think about the strategies I will use when I am learning something new or completing a task.	☆☆☆☆☆
2. I monitor my progress and adjust my strategies if they are not working.	☆☆☆☆☆
3. When something is challenging, I don't give up.	☆☆☆☆☆
4. I use my time well and don't become distracted.	☆☆☆☆☆
5. I love to learn new things.	☆☆☆☆☆
6. I ask for feedback from different sources, such as my teachers and peers, and use this feedback to make improvements.	☆☆☆☆☆
7. I understand my strengths and weaknesses as a learner.	☆☆☆☆☆
8. I know that the more effort I apply, the better my results will be.	☆☆☆☆☆

Table 4.2: Self-regulating learning reflection

1. Rate your learning experience today. (1 being the worst)(0 point)

   1 0
   2 0
   3 1
   4 9
   5 6

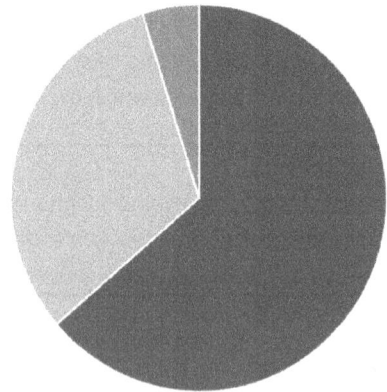

2. Did you know what was expected from you at the start of the lesson? (0 point)

   ▪ Yes 16

       No 0

3. Rate how well you participated in the lesson. (1 being the worst)(0 point)

       1 0

   ▪ 2 0

   ▪ 3 5

   ▪ 4 7

   ▪ 5 4

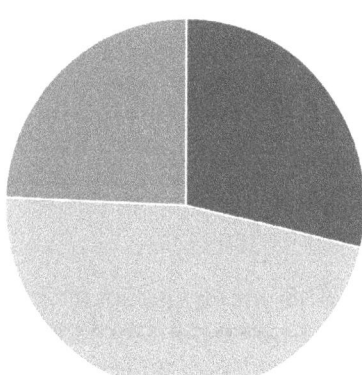

Figure 4.1: Visual representation of student engagement

Another consideration is the student question prompts adapted from Walsh and Sattes (2011) which can be used to support the development of metacognitive behaviours and self-regulating learning. The practical questions are useful in guiding students' thinking to help develop the inner language of metacognition (Wills, 2023). As always, teachers should adapt the questions according to their own contexts and the age of their students.

Question prompts:

1. What do I want to learn or be able to do?
2. What do I already think and know about this topic? Is this accurate? How do I know?
3. What strategies will I use to make meaning of the content?

4. In what ways am I monitoring my progress and understanding of the content?

5. In what ways am I taking responsibility for my own learning?

6. What have I learned? How can I take my learning to the next level? What will I do differently next time?

A memorable example of strong self-regulation was a conversation I had with a young student named Florence recently. The general gist of the conversation went something like this:

Me: What are you learning?

Florence: I'm in year 2 and we're learning about fractions. I need to be able to identify quarters in shapes and collections.

Me: How are you going?

Florence: At the moment, I can identify quarters in shapes but not collections, so that's what I'm working on.

She then went on to describe the types of activities that she was engaging in during lessons.

This young student clearly knew what the learning goal was and was able to articulate it in words that she understood. She knew exactly where she was in terms of achieving the goal and was able to identify the personal goal that she needed to work on. The main reason why this student was able to do this was because her teacher had created and continually communicated a clear learning pathway for the students in their class. The teacher had created a clear 'roadmap' for where the class was heading.

For students to articulate their learning progress in the way that Florence did, the following actions should be considered:

1. Creating and communicating a clear learning pathway

2. Show the connection between class activities and learning goals

3. Use assessment as a tool for progress monitoring

4. Build routines for self-reflection and goal setting

5. Utilise student voice and feedback

Create and communicate a clear learning pathway

Students benefit from a transparent roadmap that shows them the learning goals and the incremental steps along the way to make learning visible. As previously discussed, students need to know what they are going to learn in each lesson, how it builds on their previous knowledge and skills and why it is important for their future learning and development. This helps them to see the purpose and relevance of their learning and to monitor their own progress and achievement. Moreover, when students are clear on the expectations of the learning goals, they have a better chance of using feedback accurately.

Creating a clear learning pathway utilises the foundational skills and knowledge previously identified by the teacher teams as necessary for students to achieve mastery of the priority learning goals. Here, teachers break down complex concepts into smaller, achievable milestones that scaffold students' learning and confidence. It is essential that students understand what is expected for each milestone and can articulate this in their own words. It may mean that particular words or terms need to be explained in more detail or in simpler terms without compromising the cognitive demand of the goal. It may even mean that the cognitive verbs themselves need to be translated into student-friendly language or exemplars provided of how the cognitive verb has been demonstrated. For example, the verb 'explain' – what do we want students to DO when they 'explain' and how is 'explain' different from 'describe'? I have found in the past that sentence-stem completion activities such as the example below aid this understanding.

> Explain and describe are similar because _____.
>
> Explain and describe are different because when we explain we _____ but when we describe we _____.

There are many ways to communicate the learning pathway to students and teachers often develop quite creative methods for doing this, such as the ladder analogy in the Figure 4.2. The incremental steps are depicted as rungs on a ladder that a cartoon character is climbing. It provides a very clear pathway of the skills that students will be developing and the steps along the way.

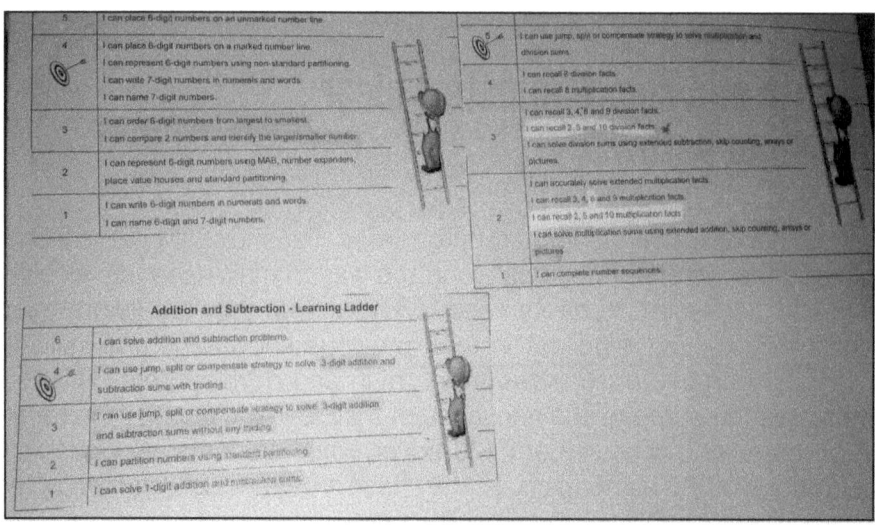

Figure 4.2: Learning ladder showing incremental milestones

Figure 4.3: Learning goal and success criteria

The example in Figure 4.3 shows where the language of the learning goal has been unpacked with the students for greater clarity. The specific success criteria that is the focus has also been highlighted. Remember that developing clarity isn't one way. Clarity is interactive and built through multiple engagements.

Co-construction is an effective way of helping students understand what is expected of them since it is an interactive process. Co-construction is the joint creation of learning pathways with students rather than simply presenting it to students and assuming they know what it means. In this process, teachers work with students to articulate what they would need to know or be able to do to achieve mastery of a target learning goal.

For example, if the goal is to understand how federal parliament operates in Australia, the incremental steps established with students might be that we need to be able to explain how people are elected to the House of Representatives and demonstrate which party/coalition forms government in a range of election scenarios. Similarly, if the goal is to understand the hierarchy of cells and the importance of cellular respiration, the learning pathway established with students might be as follows:

I can:

- recall the order of cell hierarchy
- recall the word equation for cellular respiration
- explain how body systems contribute to the process of cellular respiration

Figures 4.4 and 4.5 show anchor charts where a teacher, along with their students, has provided examples of how verbs such as infer and predict can be demonstrated. They provided specific examples of language features and text structures for further clarity and direction. These charts were created by the students under the guidance of their teacher and the students could regularly access them as they work towards achieving their learning goals.

Figure 4.5: Text features and structure

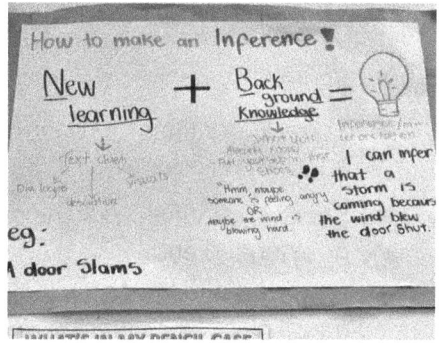

Figure 4.4: Anchor chart for inferring

Sometimes, teachers will create the learning pathway gradually over time with the students, as is the case with the example in Figure 4.6 which shows the pathway for calculating area.

It is important to keep in mind that these examples are working documents that students access over time. They are not beautifully decorated or commercially produced. Rather, they are relevant, accessible and practical, having been constructed as the unit of study or cycle of learning progresses.

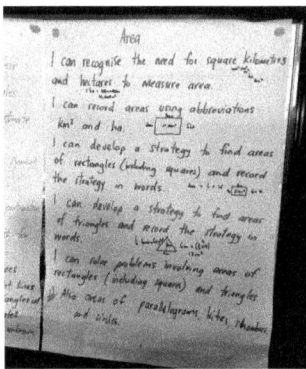

Figure 4.6: Learning pathway for calculating area developed overtime with students

Another way to show the learning pathway to students is in the format of a proficiency scale developed by Robert J. Marzano and Mark Haystead in 2008 and discussed in detail by Jan Hoegh (2020) in A Handbook for Developing and Using Proficiency Scales in the Classroom. A proficiency scale is a tool to describe a standard as a progression of knowledge. For example, a proficiency scale could show the progression of knowledge required for a year 7 student to identify the rights and responsibilities of individuals and businesses in relation to consumer as well as financial products and services.

Below I have provided a proficiency scale at a primary and secondary example linked to the Australian curriculum. You will notice the scores from 1-4.

- Score 3 represents the target prioritised learning goal,
- Score 2 identifies the prerequisite knowledge and vocabulary needed to attain mastery,
- Score 4 identifies how the student's understanding will be enriched or extended and
- Score 1 indicates that the student can demonstrate the score 2 and 3 requirements with help.

In the more complex version of a proficiency scale, half scores are also added indicating partial knowledge or understanding.

Foundation Making Connections Proficiency Scale Achievement standard:		
Make connections to personal experience when explaining characters and main events in short texts.		
Score 4.0	More complex goals	
	I can explain the connections that I have made.	
Score 3.0	The target learning goal or expectation	
	I can explain the connections that I have made.	
Score 2.0	Prerequisite skills and knowledge	
	I can recognise or recall specific terminology, such as: connection, text clue, prior knowledge.	
	I can:	
	● Tell someone about the connections I have made	
	● Talk about the main ideas (name objects, places) and characters in a text	
Score 1.0	With help, the student can meet the expectations of score 2.0 and 3.0	
	I can explain the connections that I have made.	

Figure 4.3: Foundation proficiency scale

Year 9 Drama Proficiency Scale Achievement standard:	
Use performance skills relevant to style and/or form to sustain belief, roles and characters in performances of improvised, devised and/or scripted drama for audiences.	
Score 4.0	More complex goals
	I can analyse a script to identify the subtext which will inform my vocal expression and meaningful movement.
Score 3.0	The target learning goal or expectation
	I can infer meaning from a script to inform vocal expression and movement on stage to sustain belief.
Score 2.0	Prerequisite skills and knowledge
	I can recall what the following terms mean: style, vocal expression, movement, stage directions, emotion cues, dialogue, blocking.
	I can:
	● label a script to identify character names, dialogue, stage direction, emotion cues and setting description
	● recognise how punctuation is used in dialogue to create emphasis and emotion
	● identify when I have to change my vocal expression according to emotion cues
	● use stage directions to block my movement on stage
Score 1.0	With help, the student can meet the expectations of score 2.0 and 3.0
	I can explain the connections that I have made.

Figure 4.4: Year 9 Drama proficiency scale

Communicating the learning pathway is an opportunity to make the connection between how learning goals relate to what students already know and can do. Prior knowledge connections provide students with a greater likelihood of achieving the intended learning goal, retaining new information and consolidating their knowledge. This also helps them to make connections across different subjects and disciplines and to develop a deeper and more integrated understanding.

Show the connection between class activities and learning goals

Once developed, the 'roadmap' should be referred to regularly as part of your learning routine. Students should be able to see the connections between the learning goals and classroom activities as well as how the learning goals advance their understanding of the content. This certainly isn't a time-consuming process. Rather it is simply a process of highlighting the focus of the lesson and how the students will engage in the activities that connect to the learning goals. Teachers might also build in a reference to previous lessons and then segue to the day's learning goal – *last lesson we focused on…, today we will continue our learning by focusing on…*

When students see the connection between what they're doing in class and the bigger picture, they stay motivated and engaged.

At the beginning and end of each lesson, check for students' understanding and misconceptions. During checks for understanding, remind students what they're aiming to achieve, modelling how they can check their own work against the intended outcomes and encouraging them to seek guidance about specific aspects of the work they're unclear about. This way, the checks for understanding become a powerful assessment tool for progress monitoring.

Use assessment as a tool for progress monitoring

Assessment needs to be viewed as a tool for students to understand the progress they are making and what their next steps are in the learning process. This helps students develop higher levels of self-efficacy.

Self-efficacy is how confident a person is about their ability to do a task at a certain level (Bandura, 1994). It is not about the skills a person has but how they think they can use those skills (Bandura, 1994; Jinks & Morgan, 1999; Schunk, 2012). In other words, a student may have the skills to do a task, but they may not trust that these skills are enough to do it well. Self-efficacy answers the question: can I do this? Self-efficacy influences how people think, feel, motivate themselves and act (Bandura, 2005). Therefore, this has a significant impact on motivation and academic achievement.

Students who believe in their own abilities are more likely to use better learning strategies (Walsh & Sattes, 2011). Moreover, if they experience failure, they will not attribute this to low ability, inadequacy or bad luck. Rather, they see that the failure was caused by insufficient effort or skills they still need to learn. They will also keep trying and adapting, while students who lack confidence will quit if they don't succeed at first. This starts a cycle where low self-efficacy leads to less effort, which leads to less success and even lower self-efficacy (Jinks & Morgan, 1999). Fortunately, self-efficacy can be improved in a supportive classroom environment.

One highly effective strategy is to emphasise incremental gains and celebrate progress along the way, using positive reinforcement and recognition of effort. This way students can identify that the improvements they have made and the success that they are experiencing that is related to effort. The focus changes from what students can't do to what they can do and would sound something like

> *… We are learning to tell time to the nearest minute, at the moment I can tell time to the hour and half and I'm working towards telling time to the quarter hour. I can also count in fives to 60 and I know that the lines on the clock face are one-minute intervals."*

Language such as this means that a student isn't overwhelmed by what they have to learn. Rather, they can recognise the skills that they have already developed and where they are heading next.

A characteristic that separates good teaching from highly effective teaching is the teacher's routine use of formative assessment strategies that are integrated into daily teaching practices. These assessment processes should be directly aligned to the learning goals articulated in the learning pathway so that effective feedback can be provided. This targeted feedback also helps students understand their progress and next steps.

Dylan Wiliam, a prominent figure in education, emphasises the importance of formative assessment as a powerful tool for enhancing learning and outlines five key strategies that advance learning development:

1. Clarifying, sharing and understanding learning goals and success criteria
2. Eliciting evidence of learning
3. Providing feedback that moves learning forward
4. Activating learners as instructional resources for one another
5. Activating learners as owners of their own learning

These strategies encourage clear communication of learning goals, foster engaging classroom discussions and teach students to monitor and regulate their learning through self-reflection and goal setting.

Build routines for reflection and goal setting

The capacity of students to self-reflect on the quality of their own learning plays a pivotal role in effective learning and metacognitive development. Encourage students to reflect on their learning strategies, set goals and adapt their approaches based on their understanding of their own learning process. Prompt them to think about what worked well and what they can improve. In this way, both students and teachers gain valuable insights that enable them to continuously improve. As a senior secondary teacher recently emailed me, 'It immediately identifies areas of content that need to be addressed with each particular student. When students identify that they need to do more work on the content, I can assist them in how they can achieve this (tutoring, email, textbook)'.

You might like to consider the following practical strategies:

1. **Learning Journals or Learning Logs:** encourage students to maintain a record of their learning processes, strategies and goals. Have them reflect on their learning and set both short-term and long-term goals. Revisit goals periodically so that students can monitor their progress toward their goals. Students might use sentence starters such as:

- 'Today I learnt ... and now I know...'
- 'I am still confused about ...'
- What I will do differently next time is ..."

2. **Student conferences using Two Stars and a Stair:** this strategy is adapted from a process used in a secondary school context that a school leader shared with me. Students reflect on two things they have learnt/done well, linked to the learning pathway. They also identify one thing they need to improve on (the stair). Next, the teacher discusses the two stars and one stair with the student and provides verbal feedback on what the student should focus on, to improve over the following weeks. The final step is that the student then writes down the teacher feedback on a template such as the one shown in Figure 4.7.

What is beneficial about this process is that the student must paraphrase the feedback from the teacher and record it. Often, teacher feedback is not acted upon by the students. But with this strategy, the student is required to actively engage with the feedback and process it in their own words. The completed templates are uploaded to the school's learning management system and revisited later in the term.

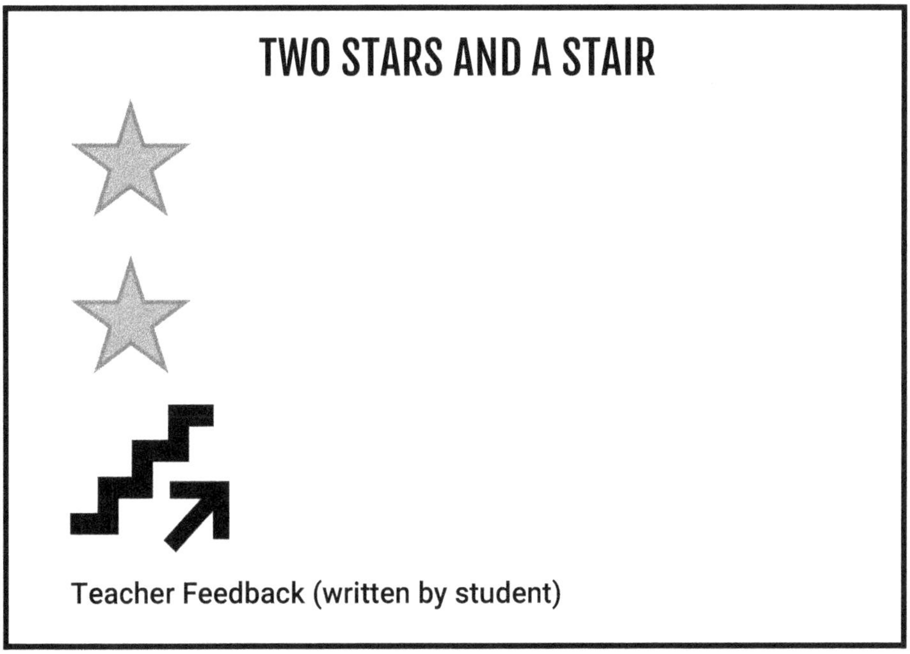

TWO STARS AND A STAIR

★

★

Teacher Feedback (written by student)

Figure 4.7: Year 9 Drama proficiency scale

3. **Glowing and growing notes** – Glowing and growing notes is a strategy for students to reflect on the goals that they have set and determine if they are achieving the goals (glowing) or still working towards them (growing). Figure 4.8 is an example from a primary school where students reflected on their learning and recorded their strengths and areas for growth. The notes that are pinned for each student show how students have recognised the growth that they made and the goals they want to achieve. One student is celebrating their ability to convert between 12- and 24-hour time while another student has identified that they need to be brave, so that they can participate in class discussions more often.

Figure 4.8: Glowing and growing student reflection

4. **Teacher reflection** – It is important for teachers to reflect on their teaching practices and the ways that they engage students in the learning process. The following questions are useful for teacher reflection and discussion. I have found them to be useful prompts as well for teachers to share ideas and strategies with one another. From here, teachers can then develop personal goals for deliberate practices to work on and improve. They often serve the purpose of highlighting the effective use of learning goals and to stop the phrase 'I already do that'. Yes, you may know about learning goals already, but do you use them in the most effective ways?

a. In what ways do I communicate learning goals so that they are clear, specific and use student friendly language?

b. When asked, are students able to identify the learning goal or topic on which they are working? Are students able to paraphrase the learning goals? How do I know?

c. In what ways do I share examples/models of student work and co-construct the learning pathway with students?

d. How do I ensure that learning goals align to curriculum expectations?

e. In what ways do I regularly refer to the learning goal throughout the lesson and make links between the goals and lesson activities or tasks?

f. How do I use formative assessment to check on and communicate learning progression?

Utilise student voice and feedback

Student voice is important. When students have the opportunity to express their thoughts, ideas and preferences, they feel empowered. Their voices contribute to decision-making processes, giving them a sense of ownership in their learning journey.

In the process of creating and communicating a clear learning pathway, it is worthwhile to ask for feedback from students in terms of what best supports their learning. Are the learning goals clear? Is the format overwhelming? What could make it more effective? Do they understand the progression of learning needed to achieve mastery of the target goals?

Recently, I was involved in a process of gaining feedback from student leaders in regard to the format proposed for communicating a learning pathway for younger students. The insights of the students were invaluable as they articulated what they liked about the format as well as changes that they would like to see made. As a result of their feedback, teachers decided to change the format of the learning pathway document from a vertical orientation to horizontal. The teachers also changed the wording of the learning stages using words such as 'working towards', 'developing', 'target' and 'enrichment'. Students also suggested a 'learning to ride a bike' analogy that teachers could use when they described the pathway to them.

They suggested that 'working towards' and 'developing' were like riding a bike with training wheels. The 'target' was riding the bike independently and 'enrichment' was riding the bike confidently in different settings.

Conclusion

Student achievement and attitude improve when they have the tools to own their learning. As educators, it's up to us to provide those tools and develop a curriculum that is ready for teachers and for students to learn it.

As Lyn Sharratt (2019) reminds us, students should be able to readily and confidently answer the following five questions:

1. What are you learning? Why?
2. How are you doing?
3. How do you know?
4. How can you improve?
5. Where do you go for help?

For students to be able to answer these questions, however, it means that teachers have:

1. deconstructed learning goals,
2. co-constructed success criteria (incremental steps),
3. given descriptive feedback,
4. used peer and self-assessment as well as set individual learning goals with students and
5. created independent, self-regulating learners.

Clarity such as this not only engages students but empowers them to take ownership of their own learning (Sharratt, 2019). 'Dragging the kids through the curriculum' isn't an option, we need to prioritise so that we can genuinely teach the essential concepts in the instructional time available. Not just cover content but enable deep understanding and knowledge application. Our students and our teachers deserve no less.

Final word

DON'T	DO
DON'T assume your teacher teams recognise the importance of creating a clear learning pathway for students.	Provide a compelling 'Why'. Design professional learning opportunities for teachers to engage with research and discuss the importance of metacognition and self-regulating learning behaviours.
DON'T use learning goals merely to comply with a directive.	Use learning goals in such a way that students are able to paraphrase the learning goal and how the goals connect to current activities within the class.
DON'T keep students in the dark.	Share the learning pathway with students and refer to it regularly so that students are clear on what they are expected to learn and why it is important.
DON'T disconnect learning from assessment.	Help students understand the progression they are making towards the identified learning goals.
DON'T underestimate the value of student input and feedback.	Ask students for feedback and input on how the learning pathways are created and communicated. What is working well? What could be improved? Most importantly, listen and act on the feedback.

Planning questions

- How will you design professional learning opportunities for teachers to engage in research regarding the development of metacognition and self-regulating learning behaviours? Why are these so important for academic success?

- In what ways might you and your teaching teams trial ways of sharing learning pathways with students?

- How will you seek student feedback to gauge the clarity of the learning pathways?

- How will you monitor the use of the learning pathways? Are they being referred to regularly during lessons and are they the basis for assessment design and differentiation?

Glossary of Terms

Term	Definition
Learning-ready curriculum	A curriculum that is learning-ready through a rigorous process of gaining clarity and agreement about the expectations, so that we are prepared to teach with set priorities, spend enough time on key concepts and have designed learning pathways so students are ready to learn it.
Cycle of learning	A unit of instruction that focuses on a particular sequence of teaching, usually focused on delivering the skills, knowledge or dispositions related to a prioritised standard or standards (Sloper & Grift, 2020).
Standards referenced reporting	Student progress is evaluated and communicated based on established learning standards.
Prioritisation process	A considered process of determining which standards need more time and focus for students to develop proficiency.
Norms	Rules or principles that define how the group members will interact, communicate and work together.
Achievement standards	Statements of what students should know and be able to do at the end of the year or two-year band. Standards (set either nationally or by state and territory curriculum authorities) provide a shared language to use when describing student achievement.
Content descriptions	Guide teachers in their understanding of the achievement standard. They specify the knowledge, understanding and skills that inform teachers about what they are expected to teach and what students are expected to learn in order to progress.
Learning goal	A statement of what students are expected to know or be able to do. It emphasises the declarative and/or procedural knowledge students will potentially gain.
Prioritised standard or content	These form the basis of the agreed and focused curriculum. They are the standards/content that teacher teams have determined as essential, requiring more time for students to master them. These will be continually monitored and assessed.
Procedural knowledge	Skills or processes that students will be able to perform that demonstrate understanding of the target content.
Declarative knowledge	Informational knowledge that students will understand in relation to the target content.
Learning pathway	A tool that communicates learning expectations and details the progression of learning needed to achieve mastery of a standard.

Co-construction	Interactive process whereby the learning pathway is jointly developed with students using student-friendly language.
Target learning goal	Statement of knowledge or skills students need to demonstrate mastery of a standard. They are derived from the prioritised achievement standards.
Prerequisite knowledge and skills	Knowledge and basic processes that build to the cognitive level of the achievement standard or target learning goal and required for students to achieve mastery.
Academic vocabulary	Highly specialised words that are related to a specific discipline. It may also include cognitive verbs such as compare, analyse, justify, etc.
Enrichment	Moving a student already demonstrating proficiency of a standard to a higher level of skills and knowledge, which is often drawn from the curriculum for the following year or level.
Metacognition	Metacognition involves being aware of our cognitive processes, learning strategies and understanding. It's about reflecting on how we approach tasks, monitor our progress and evaluate outcomes.
Self-regulated learning	Refers to a student's use of metacognitive, motivational and behavioural processes and the degree to which they take ownership of their learning.
Self efficacy	Self-efficacy refers to an individual's belief in their own capability to succeed in specific situations or to achieve particular goals.

REFERENCES

Australian Curriculum, Assessment and Reporting Authority (ACARA). (2022). *Mathematics: F-10 curriculum.* https://v9.australiancurriculum.edu.au/

Australian Curriculum, Assessment and Reporting Authority (ACARA). (2022). *English: F-10 curriculum.* https://v9.australiancurriculum.edu.au/

Australian Curriculum, Assessment and Reporting Authority (ACARA). (2022). *Design and Technologies: F-10 curriculum.* https://v9.australiancurriculum.edu.au/

Ainsworth, L. (2003). *Power Standards: Identifying the standards that matter most.* Lead+Learn Press.

Australian Institute for Teaching and School Leadership (AITSL). (2023). *Australian teacher workforce data: National trends.* https://www.aitsl.edu.au/research/australian-teacher-workforce-data/publications-and-data-tools/national-trends-teacher-workforce

Australian Education Act 2013 (Cth)

Australian Primary Principals Association. (2020). *Overcrowded primary curriculum: The impact on teachers and students.* https://appa.asn.au/wp-content/uploads/2020/03/Overcrowded-primary-curriculum.pdf

Baker, L. (2010). Metacognition. In *International Encyclopedia of Education* (Vol. 3, pp. 204–210). https://doi.org/10.1016/B978-0-08-044894-7.00484-X

Bandura, A. (1994). Self-efficacy. In V. S. Ramachaudran (Ed.), *Encyclopaedia of human behaviour* (Vol. 4, pp. 71–81). Academic Press.

Bandura, A. (2005). Exercise of personal and collective efficacy in changing societies. In A. Bandura (Ed.), *Self-efficacy in changing societies* (pp 1–45). Cambridge University Press.

Baumann, J. F., & Graves, M. F. (2010). What is academic vocabulary? *Journal of Adolescent & Adult Literacy,* 54(1), 4-12. https://doi/10.1598/JAAL.54.1.1

Beck, I. L., & McKeown, M. G. (1991). Conditions of vocabulary acquisition. In R. Barr, M. L. Kamil, P. Mosenthal, & P. D. Pearson (Eds.), *Handbook of reading research* (Vol. 2, pp. 789–814). Longman.

Beck, I. L., McKeown, M. G., & Kucan, L. (2002). *Bringing words to life: Robust vocabulary instruction.* Guilford Press.

Berne, J.I., & Blachowicz, C.L. (2008). What Reading Teachers Say About Vocabulary Instruction: Voices from the Classroom. *The Reading Teacher*, 62, 314-323.

Carver, C. S., Scheier, M. F., & Fulford, D. (2008). Self-regulatory processes, stress and coping. In O. P. John, R. W. Robins, & L. A. Pervin (Eds.), *Handbook of personality: Theory and research* (3rd ed., pp. 725–742). The Guilford Press.

Clayton, H. (2016). Power Standards: Focusing on the Essential. *Making the Standards Come Alive!*, 5(4). https://justask-publications.com/

Costa, A. L. (2001). Mediating the Metacognitive. In A. L. Costa (Ed.), *Developing minds: A resource book for teaching thinking* (3rd ed). Hawker Brownlow Education.

Earp, J. (2019, November 13). Education reform, curriculum content, and deep learning. *Teacher Magazine*. https://www.teachermagazine.com/au_en/articles/education-reform-curriculum-content-and-deep-learning

Fleming, S.M., & Frith, C.D. (2014) *The Cognitive Neuroscience of Metacognition.* Springer.

Fullan, M. (2011). *The six secrets of change: What the best leaders do to help their organization survive and thrive.* Wiley.

Grift, G., Sloper, C., & De Blasio, H. (2023). *Meetings that matter: 8 essentials for making your meetings more productive.* Grift Education.

Hattie, J. A., & Timperley, H. (2007). The power of feedback. *Review of Educational Research,* 77(1), 81–112.

Heflebower, T., Hoegh, J., & Warrick, P. (2014). *A school leader's guide to standards-based grading.* Marzano Resources.

Heflebower, T., Hoegh, J., & Warrick, P. (2021). *Leading standards-based learning: an implementation guide for schools and districts.* Marzano Resources.

Hinckley, G. B. (n.d.). *Gordon B. Hinckley quotes.* https://www.azquotes.com/author/6732-Gordon_B_Hinckley

Hoegh, J. (2020). *A Handbook for developing and using proficiency scales in the classroom.* Marzano Resources.

Hobbs, L., & Porsch, R. (2021). *Teaching out-of-field: challenges for teacher education. European Journal of Teacher Education, 44(5), 601–610.* https://doi.org/10.1080/02619768.2021.1985280

Jenkins, J. R., Stein, M. L., & Wysocki, K. (1984). *Learning vocabulary through reading. American Educational Research Journal,* 21(4), 767–787.

Jinks, J., & Morgan, V. (1999). Children's perceived academic self-efficacy: An inventory scale. *The Clearing House: A Journal of Educational Strategies, Issues and Ideas,* 79(4), 24–30. https://doi.org/10.1080/00098659909599398

Locke, E., & Latham, G. (2002). Building a practically useful theory of goal setting and task motivation: A 35-year odyssey. *American Psychologist,* 57(9), 705–717. https://doi.org/10.1037//0003-066X.57.9.705

Luccock, H. E. (1961, November 8). *The Daily Reporter,* p. 1

Marzano, R. J. (2003). *What works in schools: Translating research into action.* Association for Supervision and Curriculum Development.

Marzano, R. J. (2004). *Building background knowledge for academic achievement: Research on what works in schools.* Association for Supervision and Curriculum Development.

Marzano, R. J. (2009). *Designing and teaching learning goals and objectives.* Hawker Brownlow Education.

Marzano, R. J. (2020). *Teaching basic, advanced and academic vocabulary: A comprehensive framework for elementary instruction.* Hawker Brownlow Education.

Marzano, R. J., & Haystead, M. W. (2008). *Making standards useful in the classroom.* Association for Supervision and Curriculum Development.

Marzano, R. J., Heflebower, T., Hoegh, J. K., Warrick, P., Grift, G., Hecker, L., & Wills, J. (2016). *Collaborative Teams That Transform Schools:* The Next Step in PLCs. Marzano Resources.

Marzano, R. J., & Kendall, J. S. (2007). *The new taxonomy of educational objectives* (2nd ed.). Hawker Brownlow Education.

Miller, S.P., & Hudson, P.J. (2007). Using Evidence-Based Practices to Build Mathematics Competence Related to Conceptual, Procedural, and Declarative Knowledge. *Learning Disabilities Research & Practice,* 22, 47-57. https://doi.org/10.1111/j.15405826.2007.00230.x

Organisation for Economic Co-operation and Development (OECD). (2023). Education policy outlook in Australia. *OECD Education Policy Perspectives,* no. 67. https://doi.org/10.1787/ce7a0965-en

Papadopoulos, T. (2022, June 20). *Teaching Australia's painful shared history.* Education Matters. https://www.educationmattersmag.com.au/teaching-australias-painful-shared-history

Porta, T. (2024). *The dance of differentiation: Choreographing inclusive learning in schools.* Amber Press.

Popham, M. J. (2003). *Test better, teach better.* The instructional role of assessment. Association for Supervision and Curriculum Development.

Queensland Curriculum & Assessment Authority. (2024). https://www.qcaa.qld.edu.au/p-10/aciq/version-9/cognitive-verbs-in-version-9.0/cognitive-verb-resources

Risemberg, R., & Zimmerman, B. J. (1992). Self-regulated learning in gifted students. *Roeper Review,* 15(2), 98–101. https://doi.org/10.1080/02783199209553476

Schunk, D. H. (2001). Social cognitive theory and self-regulated learning. In B. J. Zimmerman & D. H. Schunk (Eds.), *Self-regulated learning and academic achievement: Theoretical perspectives* (2nd ed., pp. 125–151). Lawrence Erlbaum Associates.

Schulman, L. S. (2004). *The Wisdom of Practice: Essays on teaching, learning and learning to teach.* Jossey-Bass.

Schunk, D. H. (2012). *Learning theories: An educational perspective* (6th ed.). Allyn & Bacon.

Sharratt, L. (2019). *Clarity: What matters most in learning, teaching and leading.* Corwin.

Sinek, S. (2009). *Start with why: How great leaders inspire everyone to take action.* Penguin Publishing Group.

Stahl, S.A. (1986). Three Principles of Effective Vocabulary Instruction. *The Journal of Reading,* 29, 662-668.

Sternberg, R. J., Jarvin, L., & Grigorenko, E. L. (2011). *Explorations in giftedness.* Cambridge University Press.

Sloper, C. & Grift, G. (2020). *Collaborative teams that work: The definitive guide to cycles of learning in a PLC.* Hawker Brownlow Education.

Tamblyn T., Grift, G., Lipscombe, K., Sloper, C., & Wills, J. (2023). *Transformative collaboration: Five commitments for leading a professional learning community.* Grift Education.

Texas Elementary Principals & Supervisors Association's TEPSA News, August 2016, Vol. 73, No. 4, www.tepsa.org

The Conversation (2015, June 4). *Five challenges for science in Australian primary schools.* https://theconversation.com/five-challenges-for-science-in-australian-primary-schools-42413

The Conversation (2021, July 5). *Setting goals to beat previous efforts improves educational outcomes and the gains are bigger for disadvantaged students.* https://theconversation.com/setting-goals-to-beat-previous-efforts-improves-educational-outcomes-and-the-gains-are-bigger-for-disadvantaged-students-163073

Walsh, J. A., & Sattes, B. D. (2011). *Thinking through quality questioning: Deepening student engagement.* Hawker Brownlow Education.

Watson, V. (2004). *Principles of effective practice in supporting students to become self-regulated learners.* Paper Presented at NZARE Conference, Turning the Kaleidoscope, Wellington, New Zealand. https://www.nzcer.org.nz/sites/default/files/downloads/14343.pdf

White, M.A. (1968). The view from the pupil's desk. *Urban Review, 2,* 5-7. https://doi.org/10.1007/BF02350529

Wiliam, D. (2017). *Embedded formative assessment* (2nd ed.). Solution Tree Press.

Wills, J. (2023). *Thinking protocols for learning.* Grift Education.

APPENDIX A

Template for recording priority standards and content

LEARNING AREA:

STRAND:

Standard	Content Description	Prerequisite knowledge	Longevity	Context	Opportunity	Priority	Supporting
		Is this knowledge or a skill that students will need for future learning?	Is this knowledge or a skill that students will require beyond this cycle of learning, test or unit of work?	Is this knowledge or a skill that our students typically require more or less time to gain proficiency?	Will our students be disadvantaged in the future if they don't master this standard?		

APPENDIX B

Six Steps for Teaching Academic Vocabulary

(Adapted from Marzano and Pickering, 2005)

Step One: Provide a student-friendly description

The teacher provides a student-friendly description, explanation or example of the new term. Make it conversational, not a dictionary style definition.

Step Two: Students restate the description

Students restate the description, explanation or example of the new term in their own words. For the meanings to be stored in long-term memory, students must process information actively and repeatedly. The key is restating in their own words. Copying the teacher's definition/explanation won't be as effective.

Step Three: Image creation

Ask students to construct a picture, symbol or graphic representing the term or phrase. To store information in permanent memory, it must have linguistic (language) and non-linguistic (imagery based) representations.

Step Four: Periodic review

Engage students periodically in activities that help them add to their knowledge of vocabulary terms.

- highlight a prefix, suffix or root that might help them remember the word
- compare terms
- identify synonyms or antonyms
- classify words and/or list related words
- generate analogies and/or metaphors

Step Five: Discussion of terms

Students examine the entries in their vocabulary notebooks to make changes, deletions and additions. This can be done in pairs or small groups.

Students might:

- compare their descriptions of the term
- describe their pictures to each other
- explain to each other any new information they have learned or new thoughts they have had since the last time they reviewed the terms
- identify areas of disagreement or confusion and seek clarification.

Step Six: Academic games

Involve students periodically in academic games to review key terms. Set aside time each week to play games or use them spontaneously throughout the day to energise students and guide them in the review and use of important terms.

Some great examples of vocabulary games to develop content knowledge can be found at https://www.edutopia.org/article/vocabulary-games-content-knowledge

APPENDIX C

Name: _____

ONE TO FIVE

From 1 (not at all!) to 5 (aced it!) How well did you understand today's lesson?

1 **2** **3** **4** **5**

Not at all   Aced it!

What could you have done today to help yourself learn better?

Name: _____

SIMILARITIES AND DIFFERENCES

_____ and _____ are similar because they both

- _____

- _____

_____ and _____ are different because

- _____ is _____ while _____ is _____

- _____ is _____ while _____ is _____

www.ingramcontent.com/pod-product-compliance
Lightning Source LLC
Chambersburg PA
CBHW062133160426
43191CB00013B/2282